Fu Zhongwen

Mastering Yang Style Taijiquan

Fu Zhongwen

Mastering Yang Style Taijiquan

Translated by

Louis Swaim

North Atlantic Books
Berkeley, California

Fu Zhongwen: Mastering Yang Style Taijiquan

Published by
North Atlantic Books
P.O. Box 12327
Berkeley, California 94712

Cover photo of Yang Chengfu (seated) and Fu Zhongwen (standing), 1932, and all interior photos courtesy of LeRoy Clark
Cover and book design by Paula Morrison

Printed in the United States of America

Fu Zhongwen: Mastering Yang Style Taijiquan is sponsored by the Society for the Study of Native Arts and Sciences, a nonprofit educational corporation whose goals are to develop an educational and crosscultural perspective linking various scientific, social, and artistic fields; to nurture a holistic view of arts, sciences, humanities, and healing; and to publish and distribute literature on the relationship of mind, body, and nature.

Library of Congress Cataloging-in-Publication Data
Fu, Zhongwen.
    [Yang shih t'ai chi ch'uan. English]
    Fu Zhongwen: Mastering Yang Style Taijiquan /
[translated by] Louis Swaim.
    p. cm.
    Includes bibliographical references.
    ISBN 1-55643-318-2 (alk. paper)
    1. Yang, Ch'eng-fu, 1883–1936. 2. T'ai chi ch'uan. I. Swaim, Louis,
1953–   . II. Title.
    GV504 .F813 1999
    613.7'148—dc21

                                                       99-35849
                                                        CIP

2 3 4 5 6 7 8 9 / 03 02 01

Dedication

My first Taijiquan sifu used to say, "I can give you a glass of water to drink, but I cannot describe its taste." What he gave has had a lasting and profound influence on me. Perhaps in a small way this book translation is an indication that I am still drinking from that glass of water. With deep respect and gratitude, I dedicate this book to Master Kwong Gate Chan, whose way becomes a way in the walking.

> Flowing from its source it becomes a gushing spring,
> What was empty slowly becomes full;
> First turbid and then surging forward,
> What was murky slowly becomes clear.
> —D. C. Lau and Roger T. Ames, trans., *Huainanzi*, Chapter 1.

Acknowledgments

I wish to express my gratitude to the friends, family, and fellow practitioners who helped to make this project possible. While acknowledging their many suggestions and comments, I claim responsibility for any lingering errors or oversights.

Al Simon, a seasoned practitioner and teacher, read an early draft, offering helpful encouragement and pointed feedback on crucial wording in the Classics translations. Al in fact helped to steer me toward seriously translating Taijiquan materials when he engaged me several years ago in a productive dialogue about the "threading" imagery used in the Taijiquan Classics. Mr. Ruu Chang, a fellow participant at a Yang Zhenduo seminar, brought his native Chinese language skills, editorial eye, and Taijiquan proficiency to bear in reading a partial draft. I owe him a great debt for his economical but effectual comments. He helped me see the need to dig deeper on some crucial terminology, in particular the *xu ling ding jin* phrase appearing in the "Taijiquan Treatise." Alan Kasten urged me on very early in the process and generously offered useful guidance on syntactical road-mapping issues in the Classics. Stephen J. Goodson engaged me in frequent spirited debate over Taijiquan terminology and theory. LeRoy Clark kindly shared his Yang family photos. I wish to thank Richard Grossinger and the staff and associates of North Atlantic Books. Jess O'Brien deftly managed the project with heartening enthusiasm. Kathy Glass did an admirably scrupulous copyedit. Paula Morrison created a splendid design. Others who helped in numerous ways include Dave Barret, Bruce Ching, David Coulter, Jim Fox, Master Fu Shengyuan, Howin Fung, Lis Hoorweg, Fontane Ip and Brett Wagland, Jerry Karin, Ted W. Knecht, Peter Lim, Horacio Lopez, my *tongxue* Dr. Benjamin Tong, Bill Walsh, and Don Wycoff (for the computer equipment). Finally, my wife Glory and daughter Emma endured my disproportionate preoccupation and my piles of books, dictionaries and manuscript—through it all they sustained me with their love.

Table of Contents

Translator's Introduction

This book translation began as a personal exercise. I was initially attracted to Fu Zhongwen's handbook on Taijiquan because it so clearly presented the traditional Yang form that I had been practicing for more than twenty years. Much of the subject matter of the text was familiar, and yet I found that in reading it, I gained valuable perspective in my approach to studying the Taijiquan form. I began to experiment with rendering a few selected passages into English. When I shared these passages with other practitioners and friends, their reactions and encouragement spurred me on to translate the entire text in a more systematic way. Not only did I derive enormous satisfaction from this endeavor, but as it took shape, it became more and more evident that this effort was worth sharing. It is my hope that Taijiquan practitioners and teachers will welcome this translation as a valuable source book in the art of Taijiquan.[1]

Why Translate Fu Zhongwen's Book?

Fu Zhongwen is less well known in the United States than are other Chinese Taijiquan masters. He was only able to travel outside of the People's Republic of China late in life. He finally had an opportunity to visit and teach in the United States in the summer of 1994, shortly before his death in Shanghai in September of that year at the age of 91.[2] His fame in East Asia, however, is well-established, and his book, *Yang Shi Taijiquan* (Yang Style Taijiquan), published in 1963, has long been considered an essential source on the art, both in China and in overseas Chinese-speaking communities.

Fu was a disciple of Yang Chengfu (1883–1936), the eminent consolidator and standard-bearer of the art who introduced Taijiquan to thousands of students in China in the 1920s and '30s. Fu's apprenticeship began at the age of nine, and he dedicated his life to practicing and preserving the Yang Family Style of Taijiquan as taught by Yang Chengfu. He was praised by another of Yang Chengfu's famous disciples, Chen Weiming, for passing on their teacher's art unaltered. Yang Zhenji and Yang Zhenduo, Yang Chengfu's second and third sons (who continue teaching Taijiquan in China and internationally), have both acknowledged Fu Zhongwen's great contributions to the art. During an interview, Yang Zhenji said of Fu Zhongwen's book that "each movement, each posture" is depicted according to the way his father taught the form in the past, "with no alterations to the fixed postures."[3]

The book's detailed practical form instructions are based upon Fu's more than twenty years of first-hand study with Yang Chengfu. The line-art drawings that accompany the text were rendered from photos taken of Yang Chengfu's form. Together, the drawings and form instructions constitute some of the best documentation that we have of Master Yang Chengfu's art.

Special Features of the Book

In addition to Fu Zhongwen's brief preface, the book includes a historical synopsis of Yang Family Taijiquan by the famous martial arts historian Gu Liuxin, himself a former student of Yang Chengfu. Although many advances have been made in Taijiquan history since Gu wrote this essay, I include it here without comment, beyond pointing out that while the essay in its broad outlines is interesting and informative, it is clearly a product of the political times in which it was written, as can be seen in Gu's apparent need to express the value of Taijiquan in terms of its appeal to "the masses." The two essays that follow are famous direct records of the teachings of Yang Chengfu. These have been available in English translations for some time, but their content is well worth revisiting, and I hope that my effort here has yielded some of the nuances of the original texts.

The main body of the book, of course, is made up of Fu Zhongwen's form instructions. Not meant to be a "teach yourself" approach to Taijiquan, the book is rather a handbook for the more advanced student or teacher who has already learned the form and who wishes to investigate the finer levels of detail in this always-challenging art. The instructions are designed to work together with the line drawings, so that the reader has a ready visual reference for each sequence. The directional arrows help the reader to visualize the ensuing transitions. The *Important Points* that follow each sequence of instructions give insights into essential features of alignment and movement, always stressing the fundamental principles as transmitted in the "Taiji Classics." Together, these elements provide an objective framework for independent study and analysis of one's form.

Some practitioners may feel that Fu's approach is overly prescriptive and may find his repeated admonitions somewhat at odds with the way they have learned the form. I can only respond that this approach is representative of traditional methods of teaching. This is not to say that the method herein is the only way to teach, or the only way to perform Taijiquan. Certainly there are many styles of Taijiquan, and even within what is called Yang Style Taijiquan, there are many variations. Among those variations, one would be hard-pressed to say definitively what is "orthodox." What is important to keep in mind is that even though Fu Zhongwen's description of, say, White Crane Displays Wings, or Turn Body Sweep Lotus, may differ in some detail from the way that you have learned it, one can still benefit from studying his descriptions, which inevitably give insights into how to incorporate Taiji principles into one's own form. More importantly, one can gain inspiration from Fu's rigorous standard of analysis, and thereby raise one's own watermark for individual practice.

One feature of Fu's book that is relatively unknown to Taijiquan practitioners in the West is his discussion of energy points (*jindian*). Fu presents the notion of *jindian* within the wider context of "moving energy" as prescribed in the "Taiji Classics." The reader should not mistake the *jindian* for acupuncture points of traditional meridian theory. Rather, the *jindian* are points of focus or concentration that help the practitioner visualize the pathways (*jin lu*) classically referred to as "rooted in the feet, issued by the legs, governed by the waist, and expressed in the fingers." Fu provides very specific guidelines for these points of concentration for the Grasp Sparrow's Tail sequence. One can then extrapolate from this essential foundation to other areas of the form. Given Fu's remarks in the preface about the book's contents being based upon his teacher's oral instructions, there is every reason to believe that this notion of *jindian* came to him directly from Yang Chengfu. Indeed, the fact that Yang Zhenji's book, *Yang Chengfu Shi Taijiquan* (Yang Chengfu Style Taijiquan), has a similar discussion of *jindian* would seem to reinforce the idea that his father was the common source of this unique terminology.[4]

One way of understanding the *jindian* is to view them as the changing points of contact with an opponent or a partner in push-hands practice. It is for this reason that Fu Zhongwen explains the *jindian* in the context of the Grasp Sparrow's Tail sequence, since the postures of that sequence form the basis of push-hands partner practice. We are often told to imagine that we are engaging an opponent during solo practice, and the *jindian*, as presented by Fu, help the practitioner to sharpen his or her focus in this regard. Naturally, the *jindian* take on added significance in actual push-hands practice, giving practitioners helpful guidelines for raising the standards of their technique.

This brings us to another special feature of Fu Zhongwen's book that warrants some discussion. Fu tells us in his preface that he has chosen not to stress the martial arts features of Taijiquan, and he has left out any description of martial applications. Indeed, he gives only the merest hints of application potential in his bare-bones summaries of push hands and *Dalu* practice. Given the fact that Fu was a highly accomplished martial artist, and that he taught Taijiquan as a martial art—not merely as a health exercise—I can only speculate as to why he decided to take this approach in his book. Again, for a possible partial explanation, one might consider the political climate in which it was written.

Historically, the martial arts have been viewed with some ambivalence by China's government. While on one hand seen as a source of national pride and a means of improving the health and vigor of the masses, the martial arts were also traditionally viewed with suspicion as potentially posing a subversive threat. Many lament the watering-down of the traditional martial arts in their appropriation by the government to become *Guo Shu*—the "arts of the nation." Forms have been shortened, simplified, assembled into hybrids by committee, all in the interest of packaging the martial arts as a kind of exhibition sport rather far removed from their traditional origins.[5] One has to wonder, however, if Taijiquan would have survived in China at all if not for the pains taken by devotees to present the art in a way that was palatable to the Party. Indeed, I remember reading an anecdote about a Chinese Communist Party official in the late 1950s, who explained his daily Taiji practice by stating that it helped him to "resolve his internal contradictions." While cloaked in the obligatory language of Maoist dialectics, the remark must have come across to his fellow practitioners as a marvelous inside joke.

Perhaps, though, there is a more straightforward explanation for the lack of martial emphasis in Fu's book. The book, after all, is only meant to supplement the guidance of a competent instructor, and martial applications are properly the province of personal instruction. Moreover, Taijiquan is not the kind of martial art whose applications can be broken down into specific elementary techniques against specific kinds of hypothetical attacks. It is rather an art that teaches one, gradually, through individual and partner training, to respond with sensitivity to circumstances—to be able to turn an adversary's force to his or her disadvantage, while using the least possible amount of force oneself. It would appear that Fu Zhongwen's objective in this book was to elucidate the basics so that practitioners can build a foundation for such an art.

Translation Issues

Anyone who has studied a foreign language knows that, even if one reaches a level of competence allowing one to read for meaning, rendering that meaning into one's own language is an entirely separate process. Additionally, in translating materials on Taijiquan, one comes up against some particular challenges. First of all, one must gain a command of Chinese anatomical terms, as well as terms used for body-mechanical description, directionality, and positioning. Secondly, the art of Taijiquan is rich with nomenclature and vocabulary that is unique to the tradition, and this specialized language usage may be considered to be a field of study in itself. Many of the form names, for example, draw upon abiding themes in Chinese mythology and legend, while others borrow the poetic import of natural imagery. Some specialized Taijiquan vocabulary even fostered the invention of new Chinese characters, or the use of rare characters in contexts specific to the art. Moreover, the body of texts collectively referred to as the "Taiji Classics" presents its own set of challenges, being written in a highly economical form of Classical Chinese, full of idiomatic usages and allusions to philosophical, cosmological, and self-cultivation traditions. I will address these issues at greater length in the "Translator's Notes to the Taijiquan Classics." Finally, in translating any text, one must try to acquaint oneself with the *voice* of the author, and to reach a level of comfort with the author's distinctive ways of expression. In the case of Fu Zhongwen, his form instructions are very clear and straightforward, but with a profound (at times almost tedious) level of detail, and include repeated references to classical principles.

My effort in translating this book has been to adhere as closely to the original form, organization, and meaning as possible, while at the same time striving to render it into English that reads clearly and easily. In light of the challenges alluded to above, I would like clarify some of the terms and usages encountered in the text, and to reveal some of the decisions that I made in how to best present the text. An exhaustive investigation into the special terms associated with Taijiquan is beyond the scope of this book. A discussion of the historical and particular meanings of *qi*, for example, could go on for pages and pages and still not answer all questions satisfactorily. I will not attempt to do that here.[6] Still, apart from the short definitions and descriptions of terms I've provided in the glossary, a few terms and usages do need some preliminary clarification in the context of this translation.

An appropriate term to begin with is the Chinese term that is usually translated as "waist" in Taijiquan books. The term is *yao*, which differs somewhat in its anatomical meaning from the English word "waist." In English we think of the waist as the waistline—that is, the outer periphery of the midriff region. The term *yao*, however, is more precisely understood as the small of the back, or the lumbar spine and the muscles and tissues that extend out from and surround the lumbar vertebrae. This includes the lower abdomen as a physical center of gravity, but the emphasis is on the proximal, or central point. It is very important in Taijiquan to have a clear understanding that this is what is meant when we speak of the waist. Because it has become something of a convention, I translate *yao* throughout this book as "waist." In a couple of passages, Fu enlists more modern anatomical terms meaning precisely the lumbar vertebrae.

Another important term is *kua*. This can be variously translated as the "hips," "thighs," or "inner thighs." This term is so key to kinesthetic awareness in Taijiquan usage that I use the original term throughout, sometimes following with the relevant English rendering in parentheses. Bruce Kumar Frantzis' definition of the *kua* as "the area on each side of the body extending from the inguinal ligaments through the inside of the pelvis to the top (crest) of the hip bones"[7] is very apt and helpful.

Throughout this book one encounters the terms *song* and *fang song*. These are often translated as "relaxed" and "relax." Etymologically the term *song* is based on a character for "long hair that hangs down"—that is, hair that is loosened and expanded, not "drawn up." Therefore, "loosened" and "loosen" are more accurate renderings for *song* and *fang song*. The phonetic element that gives the character *song* its pronunciation means, by itself, "a pine tree," which carries an associated imagery of "longevity," much as evergreens are associated with ongoing vitality in the West. This may provide a clue to the Taijiquan usage of this term, which must not be confused with total relaxation, but is closer to an optimal state of the condition referred to as **tonus** in English anatomical parlance; that is, the partial contraction of the musculature, which allows one to maintain equilibrium and upright posture. The aligned equilibrium that is prescribed in Taijiquan is associated with imagery of being "suspended" from the crown of the head. One can, therefore, draw upon the available imagery of both something that is loosened and hangs down, and that of the upright pine, whose limbs do not droop down, but are buoyant and lively.

Closely related to the concept of *song* is that of movement of *jin*. Taijiquan theory requires that one "use mind, not strength." This means, in part, that one should not use strength *against* an opponent, nor should one resist unyieldingly against the force of one's partner. As a result, Taijiquan theory has developed a highly idiomatic way of discussing strength and the use of strength in the art. *Jin* as it is used in Taijiquan means energy or strength that results from the integrated use of body and consciousness, in contrast to discrete muscular strength (*li*). The character for muscular strength (*li*) depicts a naked flexed arm. The character for *jin* contains the *li* element, and a phonetic component (*jing*) on the left-hand side. That component by itself means "streams running underground" or "flowing water." Sometimes elements that were chosen as a phonetic were also chosen for meaning, and this character seems to connote strength or energy that flows as a stream. An early usage of this character from the Warring States period is for the collective strength of troops. This is suggestive in itself if one considers the criteria: Not one soldier working alone—not a bunch of soldiers working independently—rather, many soldiers working together as a unit, coordinated, with effective lines of communication, well-led. This is a splendid model for the efficient body mechanics required in Taijiquan. An important Taiji Classic, Li Yiyu's "Five-Character Formula," says that "*Jin* is integrated. The *jin* of the whole body is trained to become one family." The emphasis, then, is not upon strength, but upon its integration, its adaptability, and its appropriate use in yielding and responding.

The word *jin* is often used in compounds such as *pengjin* (ward-off energy), *lujin* (roll-back energy), *jijin* (press energy), *anjin* (push energy), etc., that imply an application of integrated strength with specific directionality and technique. In this sense it is a specific quality of kinetic energy, or energy associated with movement. But if we define *jin* simply as a type of strength or technique, it is difficult to account for its Taijiquan usages in nominal phrases such as *tingjin* (listening energy), or *dongjin* (comprehending energy).[8] For this reason, I define the Taijiquan usage of this word *jin* as **integrated strength/sensitivity**. The word "sensitivity" helps to connote the vital element of consciousness, or mind intent (*yi*), so key to the notion of *jin*.

Turning to particular usages that Fu Zhongwen incorporates in his form descriptions, we see that one especially effective device is his solution to the problem of how to describe the rotational arm movements that accompany the shifting of weight and turning of the torso during the course of the form. These movements are what are referred to as the "turning transitions" in the "The Mental Elucidation of the Thirteen Postures." With succinct anatomical description of the interaction of the radius and ulna in the forearm, Fu establishes a convention for depicting the rotation of the arm inward and outward. In my experience, this descriptive convention may appear rather counter-intuitive for some people until it has been absorbed over time. For that reason, I have placed the words **rotate** and **rotation** in bold type throughout the text to help focus the reader's attention on this important detail. Fu additionally provides clarifying language in almost every case as to where the palm faces, from beginning to end, in a given sequence. This kinesthetic detail is a crucial component of the integrative attribute in Taijiquan movement.

A perennial challenge in the verbal description of Taijiquan movement is how to depict movements that are synchronous with language that is linear and sequential. Fu handles this in several ways. Often he describes one set of weight-shifting movements or torso-turnings, then proceeds to describe the attendant arm and leg movements with the transitional words "at the same time" or "concurrently." In like manner, many of his descriptions contain the words "gradually," "slightly," "continuing," "according with," and "following," thereby emphasizing the processional quality of the movements. Fu, for example, never tells us simply to "move into a forward bow stance," but instead guides the reader repeatedly through every transitional detail as the weight gradually shifts onto the forward leg, finally "forming a left bow stance."

Another device that Fu uses for depicting synchronous, processional movement, is a syntactical stratagem of Chinese grammar that is difficult to replicate in English. This syntactical convention has been called the "durative aspect," a way of signaling the ongoing nature of an event.[9] One of the ways this is done in Chinese is by using a grammatical particle, *zhe*, after the verb, marking its durative aspect. Fu enlists this stratagem countless times to depict integrated sets of motion, usually with the initial verb, "follow" (*sui*), then the main action verb, followed by *sui* again with the *zhe* particle, then the verb for the attendant action. Here, *sui* is not actually read as "follow" or "following." Instead, it conveys the meaning of, "In the course of doing action **x**, action **y** is done concurrently." Accordingly, I've rendered these types of sentences as, "While deflecting, the arm rotates out, causing the palm to face in." In other sentences, Fu uses the same verb, "follow" (*sui*), but without the durative particle. Here the reading is, "Following the turning of the body, the right palm moves up in an arc." In this case, while some sequential ordering of actions is implied (the waist *leads* the movement), it is important to understand that he is describing synchronous movement; that is, *following* here means following *with*.

Fu uses a number of terms that require additional explanation. One of these is the term for what is typically called the ending postures of the forms, that is, the terminus point of a given posture such as White Crane Displays Wings. The term that Fu uses for these ending postures is *dingdian*, or "fixed points." In Taijiquan, however, "fixed points" are not really fixed, and "ending postures" are not really the end of anything. Fu therefore advises the reader that "as each movement reaches a fixed point (*dingdian*), one must accomplish what is called 'seems to stop, does not stop'." The *dingdian*, then, must be understood to be both the culmination of one sequence as well as the beginning of the next.

In speaking of the shifting of the body from one leg to the other, Fu makes constant reference to the center of gravity (*zhongxin*). Although closely related in location and concept, this should not be confused with the *dantian*, the point of concentration below the navel to which the practitioner is directed to "sink the *qi*." The *zhongxin* is more properly a way of talking about the body's physical center of gravity.

Fu also employs some very interesting verbs to describe the footwork and stances of Taijiquan. To form a bow stance (*gongbu*), he tells us that the front leg is bent or "bowed" (*gong*), while the rear leg "treads" (*deng*) to the rear. In some cases I have translated this as "treads," as it suggests the importance of maintaining an evenly distributed pressure with the entire surface area of the foot. Elsewhere in the book, I have translated this as "the rear leg pushes from the heel," which I think better captures the intended meaning of progressive movement, but the reader should always bear in mind the "treading" of the foot mentioned here. Another interesting verb is used to describe a foot as it transforms from a partially-weighted to a fully-weighted condition, or from a condition where the weight-bearing surface changes from the heel or ball of the foot to the entire sole of the foot. For this Fu uses the word *ta*, which I translate "to plant": "Using the heel as the pivot, follow the turning of the body until the toes have turned in as far as possible, then plant the foot."

An Authentic Handbook

In his preface, Master Fu Zhongwen tells us that "to the best of my ability I have written in accordance with the requirements for each posture as advanced by my former teacher in his verbal instructions to me; I've neither added nor taken away." The art of Taijiquan was long a closely guarded body of secrets handed down from master to student. The teachings of subtle and profound philosophy, medical and cosmological theory, and rigorous physical training were carefully conveyed in oral tradition. In the rare cases when teachings were written down, they were kept as family manuals, and not shared with outsiders. This situation only began to change early in this century, when the "Taiji Classics" were first made available to the public, and modern masters began to publish books on the theory and practice of the art. In this tradition, Fu Zhongwen has left us an authentic handbook, capturing the distinctive features of Yang Style Taijiquan in a clear and thorough presentation. With this translation, the handbook will become available to an even wider audience. It is both an important part of the Yang legacy and a useful guide for individuals pursuing mastery.

The Daoist text, the *Zhuangzi*, contains many stories of skilled artisans, craftspeople, even cooks, whose mastery of their crafts Zhuangzi holds up as a model for sagehood. In the book *Essays on Skepticism, Relativism, and Ethics in the Zhuangzi*, Lee H. Yearley examines Zhuangzi's portrayals of skillful activity and how they serve to illustrate paths to the "ultimate spiritual state."[10] Yearley identifies a number of characteristics of perfected-skill activities, one of which is,

> a special sensitivity to changing circumstances, an instantaneous
> responsiveness that accords with the general rules of an activity

but is not simply guided by them. Skillful people, that is, see and move with changes, always adapting to them, never asserting themselves against them.[11]

Yearley goes on to say that another characteristic of skillful actions is that,

although they are easier to produce than unskillful or normal action, they reach their goals more effectively than do those kinds of action. That is, a notable gain in power and efficacy occurs but it often occurs without the addition of effort. Skillful actions appear to tap a new source of power, one that generates a new flow of energy that exceeds what could be produced by either brute strength or willful application.[12]

Still another characteristic of skillful activity, says Yearley, is "the unification of the mental and the physical." Moreover,

Skillful actions with these characteristics also both arise from and manifest a personal tranquillity. That is, one must effortlessly concentrate on the activity itself, and that involves forgetting normal concerns and goals as well as possessing a settled but active mind and a stable if vigorous physical state.[13]

Finally, Yearly states, "skill activities, at least at their most refined, can make you feel part of the larger rhythm of some meaningful whole."[14]

I quote these descriptions of the characteristics of skillful activity at length because it seems to me that they reflect the appeal of the art of Taijiquan, an appeal that goes well beyond its value as a physical exercise or a martial art. The characteristics cited, in fact, sound remarkably like the characteristics and requirements expressed in traditional Taijiquan teachings, particularly as found in the "Taiji Classics." We are very fortunate to have those classic texts of early masters that point to the upper reaches of Taijiquan's "skillful activity." Those texts, however, are highly philosophical and would have little meaning if we did not have the practical instructions and guidance of more recent masters, including Fu Zhongwen, who have brought the art out of the closed courtyards and into the public parks.

Notes

1. I use the Chinese *pinyin* system of romanization for Chinese words in this book, including the words Taijiquan and Taiji. The *pinyin* system was developed by linguists in China and has been the official romanization system in the PRC since 1953. While *pinyin* has a few idiosyncrasies of its own, it is far more internally consistent then the older, cumbersome Wade-Giles system, and does a much better job of representing standard Mandarin pronunciation. Accordingly, *pinyin* has gained wide acceptance in the West as the standard for Mandarin language learning, for journalism, and increasingly for works of scholarship where Wade-Giles once held sway. Most Westerners were introduced to the name Taijiquan through the Wade-Giles spelling: T'ai-chi ch'üan. The usage in the majority of English books and publications on Taijiquan to date has been loosely based on Wade-Giles. However, actual adherence to Wade-Giles conventions has been lax, and anomalous spellings abound. For example, most titles omit the umlaut marking the raised vowel in the final syllable (in pinyin, the raised vowel in a final is indicated by the initial "q," while a non-raised vowel is indicated by the initial "ch"). Some titles omit the required hyphenation in the compound adjective-noun "T'ai-chi." Other titles are careless with the aspiration marks, omitting the needed marks either in the first syllable, "Tai," or the last, "chuan," or both. Ironically, many of us habitually mispronounce the name as though the middle syllable were aspirated, which it is not.

2. See Marvin Smalheiser, "A Last Interview with Fu Zhongwen," *T'ai Chi* magazine, Vol. 18, No. 6, December 1994.

3. In Yang Zhenji and Yan Hanxiu, *Yang Chengfu Shi Taijiquan* (Yang Chengfu Style Taijiquan), (Guangxi Minzu Chubanshe, 1993), p. 250.

4. *Ibid.,* pp. 8–9, et passim.

5. See Howard Thomas, *Tai Chi Training in China: Masters, Teachers, and Coaches,* (London: Paul H. Crompton Ltd, 1996).

6. See the helpful overview of the early conception of *qi* in Sarah Allan, *The Way of Water and Sprouts of Virtue* (Albany: State University of New York Press, 1997), pp. 87–92. One of the more interesting definitions I have found for *qi* is in Manfred Porkert, *The Theoretical Basis*

of Chinese Medicine (Cambridge, 1974), pp. 167–168. According to Porkert, *qi* "comes as close as possible to constituting a generic designation equivalent to our word 'energy.'... And yet, unlike our concept of energy, *qi*, whatever the context and absolutely without exception, always implies a qualitative determination of energy.... For this reason we use for the technical term *qi* the standard definitions 'configurational energy'—i.e., energy of a definite direction in space, of a definite arrangement, quality or structure—and 'energetic configuration'." Quoted in John Hay, "The Human Body as a Microcosmic Source of Macrocosmic Values in Calligraphy," in Kasulis, Thomas, et al., eds., *Self as Body in Asian Theory and Practice* (Albany, State University of New York Press, 1993), p. 191.

7. Bruce Kumar Frantzis, *The Power of Internal Martial Arts: Combat Secrets of Ba Gua, Tai Chi, and Hsing-I* (Berkeley: North Atlantic Books, 1998), p. 337; and Frantzis, *Opening the Energy Gates of Your Body* (Berkeley: North Atlantic Books, 1993), pp. 90–93.

8. Although *tingjin* and *dongjin* sometimes appear in contexts that suggest their usage as noun phrases, they may also be understood in the sense of listening *to* energy, or comprehension *of* energy.

9. Charles N. Li and Sandra A. Thompson, *Mandarin Chinese: A Functional Reference Grammar* (Berkeley: University of California Press, 1981), pp. 202–203, 217–226.

10. Lee H. Yearley, "Zhuangzi's Understanding of Skillfulness and the Ultimate Spiritual State," in *Essays on Skepticism, Relativism, and Ethics in the Zhuangzi*, ed. Paul Kjellberg and Philip J. Ivanhoe (Albany: State University of New York Press, 1996), pp. 152–182.

11. *Ibid.*, p. 172.

12. *Ibid.*

13. *Ibid.*, pp. 172–173.

14. *Ibid.*, p. 173.

Fu Zhongwen, 1957

Yang Luchan (1799–1872), founder of Yang Style Taijiquan

Yang Banhou (1837–1892)

Yang Jianhou (1839–1917)

Yang Shaohou (1862–1930)

Yang Zhaopeng (1875–1938)

Yang Chengfu (left) with Zhang Qinglin (driver's seat) and Zhou Bin

Fu Sheng Yuan (Fu Zhongwen's son)

Fu Zhongwen

Mastering Yang Style Taijiquan

Fu Zhongwen's Preface

The introductory essay for this book was written by Gu Liuxin and introduces in summary fashion the origins, development, and special characteristics of Taijiquan.

The two essays "A Discussion of Taijiquan Practice" and "The Ten Essentials of Taijiquan Theory" are recorded from my late teacher, Yang Chengfu's *Taijiquan Ti Yong Quan Shu* (Complete Book of the Essence and Applications of Taijiquan), and I have made a few abridgments here and there in order to provide guidance for the reader while practicing.

The illustrations of the *Taiji* sequence and of push hands are from my practice narrative and are drawn by Mr. Zhou Yuanlong.

The goal of compiling and writing this book lies in carrying on the traditional way, yet it is not from a martial arts standpoint. Therefore, I have offered a fairly detailed explanation of the movements, but omitted the martial applications. As for the Important Points of the movements, I have based them on each of the originals in *Taijiquan Ti Yong Quan Shu*. At the same time, I have consulted my former teacher's *Taijiquan Shi Yongfa* (Self-Defense Applications of Taijiquan). Moreover, to the best of my ability I have written in accordance with the requirements for each posture as advanced by my former teacher in his verbal instructions to me; I have neither added nor taken away. I share this to serve as a standard form. As for the illustrations, seventy-six of them are traced from existing photographs of my former teacher's form. The remainder were drawn and added as needed for practice method and analysis of the movements.

—Respectfully submitted by Fu Zhongwen

An Introduction to Yang Style Taijiquan

Yang Fukui, styled Yang Luchan (1799–1872), a native of Yongnian county in Hebei province, was an impoverished youth who at around ten years of age went to Chen Village in Wen county in search of a livelihood. From the Chen style boxing master, Chen Zhangxing (1771–1853), he studied the broad-framed *laojia* Chen style of Taijiquan. Then when he had reached adulthood, he returned home to pass on what he had learned, using his skills at avoiding and prevailing over the force of hardness and strength. At that time, people named this art *Zhan Mian Quan* (cotton boxing), *Ruan Quan* (soft boxing), or *Hua Quan* (transformation boxing).

Three brothers in a prominent Yongnian family, Wu Chengqing, Wu Heqing (style-named Yuxiang), and Wu Ruqing, were martial arts aficionados who also learned *Taijiquan* from Yang Luchan. Ruqing, who served as an official in the Siquan Ministry of Justice, recommended that Luchan go to the capital to teach boxing to the sons of the Qing Imperial princes. Luchan became quite famous and was appointed martial arts instructor to the imperial banner battalion.

In order to adapt to certain considerations, Luchan gradually revised the original form that included *fajin* (issuing energy), leaps, stomping of the feet, and other moves of comparative difficulty. Subsequently, his third son, Jianhou (styled Jinghu, 1839–1917), revised it to what is known as "middle frame." It further passed on to Jianhou's third son, Chengfu (1883–1936), who again revised and standardized it as the large-frame Yang Style, to distinguish it from the small-frame style taught by his uncle Yang Banhou (1837–1892). Yang Chengfu's form became the most broadly popular current style of *Taijiquan*.

4

The Yang style that developed from Chen *laojia* has a pace that is relatively even and slow, without stopping, unlike the alternating of fast and slow in Chen style, or the change between storing and issuing. The movements of Yang style are simple and straightforward; its movement of energy is like the slow circular rotations of drawing silk, different from the windings, twists, and turns (*chanrao zhuan zhe*) of Chen style, where the movement of energy is distinctly spiral, or screw-like. As for the movements and breathing being natural and unified, Yang style simply adopts the method of *qi chen dantian* "sink the qi to the *dantian*," whereas the Chen style method unites *dantian nei zhuan* "turning the *dantian* within" with *qi chen dantian*. The moderate and easy practice method of Yang style *Taijiquan* makes it easily learned by the great masses. This is an important reason for the relatively wider development and spread of Yang style compared to Chen style.

The three generations of Yang style teachers, because their martial skill enjoyed abundant fame in the North, chose, as a matter of course, young and able students, and taught them devotedly. Because of this, their disciples and students were many. Of particular note was the year 1928, when Chengfu traveled from the North to cities of the South, teaching boxing in Nanjing, Shanghai, Hangzhou, Guangzhou, Hangkou, etc. His form consequently disseminated and was practiced in all parts of the entire country.

The distinctive characteristics of Yang Chengfu style Taijiquan are: the postures are relaxed and expansive, simple and clean, precise in composition; the body method is centered and aligned, not inclining or leaning; the movements are harmonious and agreeable, containing hard and soft, uniting lightness of spirit and heaviness of application. In training, one attains softness from loosening/relaxing (*song*). In accumulating softness one develops hardness; hardness and softness benefit one another [mutually interact]. The postures may be high, middle, or low, so that one is able to make appropriate adjustments in the measure of the movements according to the factors of age differences, sex, bodily strength, or differing demands of the student. Because of this, it is as suitable for treating illness or protecting health as it is for increasing strength and fitness or increasing the artistic skill of one who is relatively strong to begin with.

The postures of Yang style Taijiquan are expansive and open, light yet heavy, natural, centered and upright, rounded and even, simple, vigorous, and dignified,—because of this, one is able to quite naturally express an individual style that is grand and beautiful.

When Yang Chengfu was actually performing his art, he followed the established guidelines with discipline. He both understood and observed the standards: light, lively, steady and calm, centered and upright, rounded and full, softness containing hardness, nimble and spirited in manner and bearing. We can see from the posture illustrations in this book that in his entire aspect he measured up to the high standards of Taijiquan's training essentials and model style.

Yang Chengfu once said: "Taijiquan is the art of softness containing hardness, of a needle concealed in cotton. The postures must be centered and upright, rounded and full, calm and steady, relaxed and tranquil; the movements are light, lively, and curved— a completely marvelous action." In actuality, this is an account of his own attainment.

After Yang Chengfu went to the South, he began to explicitly emphasize the use of *Taijiquan* in treating illness and protecting health. For example, when Chengfu first performed his art in Shanghai, the movements of Separating Feet and Kick with Heel still retained the training methods of rapid kicks having the sound of the wind. Later, however, he changed to slow, gradual kicks, with the placement of *fajin* (issuing energy) in the kicks being concealed within. Other boxing powers and methods were also transformed to a continuous pace with no breaking of the cadence, and from a hurried to an even pace.

Yang Chengfu had an extraordinarily large build. His adroitness in push hands was exquisite; his skill at neutralizing and in *fajin* was unrivaled in his time. When he put out his hand it had the softness of cotton but seemed to contain a bar of steel. It moved very slightly, reached exceedingly far, and released energy with extreme swiftness; yet whenever there was a case of receiving his issuing, before one could even feel him move, one was sent soaring and tumbling into the air. For this reason, students loved his art and found great pleasure in pursuing their studies.

Chengfu's elder brother, Shaohou (1862–1930), learned the greater portion of his boxing art from his uncle, Banhou. His character was close to the firm and contentious nature of Banhou. His boxing style was originally consistent with Chengfu's. In his later years, Shaohou began to change his form: a high frame with lively steps, movements gathered up small, alternating between fast and slow, hard and crisp *fajin*, with sudden shouts, eyes glaring brightly, flashing like lightning, a cold smile and cunning expression. There were sounds of *"heng and ha,"* and an intimidating demeanor. The special characteristics of Shaohou's art were: using soft to overcome hard, utilization of sticking and following, victorious *fajin*, and utilization of shaking pushes. Among his hand methods were: knocking, pecking, grasping and rending, dividing tendons, breaking bones, attacking vital points, closing off, pressing the pulse, interrupting the pulse. His methods of moving energy were: sticking/following, shaking, and connecting. Attackers were immediately struck down. When Shaohou was teaching his students, it didn't matter who they were, once they commenced, he would hit them. Moreover, his expressions and attitudes ranged from joy to anger. Those of shallow accomplishment imitated him with difficulty. Although his students admired his skill, they rarely were able to complete the full course of their training. Therefore, although his name was equally well known as Chengfu's, Chengfu's reputation flourished in comparison.

Chengfu's boxing style during his middle years was bold and vigorous, powerful and strong, imposing with its leaps. His student, Chen Weiming, wrote the book *Taijiquan Shu* (The Art of

Taijiquan), expounding its principles. Chengfu later asked someone to compile *Taijiquan Ti Yong Quan Shu* (Complete Book of the Essence and Applications of Taijiquan). At this time, Chengfu's body weight was 290 pounds. Yet his photos reveal a deportment that was composed, relaxed, and serene—hardness contained within softness, he had already reached the consummation of skill.

Three generations of the Yang family continuously taught *quan*, ceaselessly innovating in teaching curricula and methods, adapting to the needs of the masses. Their boxing art is the most widely disseminated.

—Gu Liuxin

Chapter One

Taijiquan Essentials

A Discussion of Taijiquan Practice

Although Chinese martial arts are divided into numerous factions, it is important to know that they all contain techniques that are based on philosophical principles. Those of our forefathers who exhausted their whole life's energies, yet were still unable to fathom its mysteries, can be seen throughout time. If students expend a day's efforts, they will obtain a day's results. As the days and months accumulate, success will come.

Taijiquan is the art of softness containing hardness, of a needle concealed in cotton. Its technique, physiology, and mechanics are imbued with considerable philosophical principles. Therefore, those who would study this method must go through definite stages and appropriate duration of time. Although the guidance of an excellent master and diligent training with friends must not be underemphasized, most important is individual daily practice. Otherwise, one can discuss it till the end of time, or think longingly for an entire year, but once you are engaged in a fight, there is a total absence of substance, and you remain a novice without a day's accomplishment (*gongfu*). The ancients said: "You can think all day with no outcome—it is not as good as study."* If you are able to practice and refine morning and night as soon as you are motivated, no matter if you are old or young, male or female, you will succeed.

Recently those studying *Taijiquan* have been spreading from the North to the South, and enthusiasts are increasing daily—this cannot help but improve the prospects of the martial arts. So, amongst

---

*Translator's Note: This is an allusion to a phrase in the Confucian *Analects*, and a similar phrase in the *Xunxi*.

enthusiasts, those students who are devoted and sincere will have a future without limits. We are definitely not lacking for students. However, it is generally impossible to avoid two routes: in the first instance are those already possessing talent, who are young and strong, can draw inferences easily, and are clever beyond the average—what a pity that they barely accomplish anything, yet are satisfied and will suddenly stop studying, unable to endure a great undertaking. In the second instance are those who impatiently seek quick results, yet who are careless in their development. Before a whole year has passed they have already studied the hand, sword, broadsword, and spear forms. Although able to imitate in rote fashion, they in fact never master the secrets. As soon as one checks their directions and movements, upper, lower, inner, and outer, all come up short. If you want to make corrections, then you must amend each and every posture. Moreover, corrections made in the morning have already been forgotten by nightfall. This is why one often hears the saying, "To study boxing is easy; to correct boxing is difficult." This saying comes from the seeking of quick results. If this present generation by means of mistakes transmits mistakes, they will certainly extend their own mistakes to others—most distressing for the future of the martial arts.

When initially learning Taijiquan, one must first study the form. Studying the form means to learn each of the postures named within the syllabus, each posture as taught by a master. The student must, with resolute mind, memorize and ponder, and practice accordingly. This is called studying the form. At this time the student should concentrate on the inner, outer, upper, and lower [aspects]. Regarding the internal then, this is what is called using the consciousness rather than strength. Below, one must sink the *qi* to the *dantian*. Above, one must experience a light and insubstantial energy at the top of the head. Regarding the exterior, the entire body is light and agile, "the joints are threaded together," from the feet to the legs to the waist. Sink the shoulders, bend the elbows, and so forth. When you begin to study Taijiquan, ponder these few sentences morning and night, memorize them until you intuitively understand them. Each posture and gesture must always be carefully analyzed; one's deportment in practice must seek what is correct. When you've completed one form completely, then work on the next. Then gradually you will reach completion in your practice. If you proceed in this manner, making corrections, with the passing of time, there will be no changes in the essential principles.

When practicing the movements, all the joints of the entire body must be relaxed, open, and natural. First, one must not inhibit the *qi* in the mouth or abdomen; second, do not allow force to gather up in the limbs, the waist, or the legs. These two ideas are expressed by various practitioners of *nei quan* (internal martial arts). However, once they commence movement, with one turn of the body or kick of the legs or swing of the waist, they gasp for air, and their bodies become agitated. These flaws come from holding the breath and adding force to the movements.

1. When practicing, the head must not incline, slant, or bend. This is what is called "The top of the head is suspended," or the idea of carrying an object on the top of one's head. Guard against rigid straightness—this is the meaning of "being suspended." Although the gaze is extended forward evenly, there are times when following the body's changes of position that the line of sight, while directed to emptiness, plays a crucial role in the transformations and supplements the insufficiencies of body and hand techniques. The mouth seems open yet not open, closed yet not closed. Breathe out through the mouth and in through the nose in a natural way. If saliva is produced beneath the tongue, just swallow it, do not spit it out.

2. The body should be centered and upwardly aligned, not leaning. The spine with the *weilu* (coccyx) hangs straight down without inclining. However, when encountering the changes of opening and closing, the activities of containing the chest and pulling up the back, sinking the shoulders and turning the waist, beginning students must pay attention. Otherwise, after a period of time cor-

rections will be difficult and one will tend toward stiffness. Even if one has put in a great deal of effort, it will be difficult to attain any benefit or use.

3. The joints in the two arms must be loosened (*song*) and open. The shoulders must hang down, the elbows must bend down, and the palms must slightly extend, with the fingertips slightly bent. Use consciousness to move the arms, use the *qi* to thread to the fingers. With the accumulation of days and months, the internal energy will be penetrating and refined; its subtlety will arise on its own.

4. You must distinguish insubstantial and substantial in the two legs, lifting and lowering them like the movements of a cat. When the body's weight shifts to the left, then the left is substantial, and the right leg is called empty. When shifted to the right, then the right leg is substantial and the left leg is called empty. What is here called empty is not void, for its power is not yet disconnected, but reserved and retained in the intention of the changes of expansion and contraction. What is called substantial is simply that it is sound and real—without excessive use of energy, which would mean use of fierce strength. Therefore, the legs bend according to the standard of vertical alignment [of the front leg's knee with the toes]. To exceed this is called excessive force, and in striking forward the body then loses its central equilibrium.

5. With regard to the feet, one must distinguish between the kicking methods of Left and Right Separate Feet, and Kick with Heel. In the former, concentrate on the toes. In the latter, concentrate on the entire sole. Where the intention reaches, the *qi* reaches; where the *qi* reaches, the *jin* will certainly follow. However, the joints of the legs must also be relaxed (*song*), open, and smooth and stable in issuing energy. At these times, it is most easy to allow a build-up of stiff energy, for the body to twist and turn in an unstable way, and the leg's kick will have no power.

The Taijiquan curriculum begins with practicing the Taiji hand set, followed by single-hand pushing circuit, fixed-step push hands, active-step push hands, *dalu*, and *sanshou*, then comes implements training, such as Taiji sword (*jian*), broadsword (*dao*), spear (*qiang*), and so forth.

Regarding practice time, each day practice twice upon getting up from bed. If there is not time in the morning, then practice twice before retiring. Within the course of a day, one should practice seven to eight times, but at least one time per day. However, avoid practicing after drinking alcohol or immediately after a meal.

As for the place of practice, a garden courtyard or large hall with good air circulation and plenty of light is suitable. Avoid direct drafts of strong wind and places that are cold, damp, and musty. Since the breathing deepens as the body undergoes exercise, strong drafts and damp air may penetrate the body to the internal organs, and one will easily fall ill. As for practice clothing, most appropriate are roomy, simply-cut clothes and broad-toed cloth shoes. If, after practice, you have been perspiring, avoid removing your clothing and exposing your skin, or washing with cold water. Otherwise you may fall ill.

—Dictated by Yang Chengfu, recorded by Zhang Hongkui

The Ten Essentials of Taijiquan Theory

1. *An intangible and lively energy lifts the crown of the head.* This refers to holding the head in vertical alignment, with the spirit threaded to the top of the head. One must not use strength; using strength will stiffen the neck and inhibit the flow of *qi* and blood. One must have the conscious intent of an intangible, lively, and natural phenomenon. If not, then the vital energy (*jingshen*) will not be able to rise.

2. *Contain the chest and raise the back.* "Containing the chest" means to hold in the chest slightly to allow the *qi* to sink to the *dantian*. One must avoid rigidity in the chest; thrusting out the chest will cause blockage in the chest cavity. One will be heavy above and light below; the heels will float up. "Raise the back" means the *qi* adheres to the back. If one is able to contain the chest, then one will naturally be able to raise the back. If one can raise the back, the strength will be able to issue from the spine, and you will be undefeatable.

3. *Relax the waist.* The waist is the body's ruler. If you are able to relax the waist, the two feet will have strength and the foundation will be stable. The changes of insubstantial and substantial all come from the turning movements of the waist, hence it is said, "The source of meaning is in the region of one's waist." If there is a situation in which you are unable to attain strength, you must seek the cause in the waist.

4. *Distinguish insubstantial and substantial.* The art of Taijiquan takes the distinction between insubstantial and substantial as the first principle. If the weight of the entire body is placed over the

right leg, then the right leg is substantial and the left leg is empty. If the entire body's weight is placed over the left leg, then the left leg is substantial and the right leg is empty. If one is able to distinguish empty and full, then the body's turning motions will be light and agile, and there will be no wasted strength. If one is unable to distinguish, one's steps will be heavy and sluggish, one's stance will be unsteady, and one will easily be unbalanced by an opponent's pull.

5. *Sink the shoulders and drop the elbows.* "Sink the shoulders" means the shoulders are relaxed, open, and allowed to hang down. If one is unable to relax and allow the two shoulders to hang down, they will rise up, then the *qi* will also follow them up, and the whole body will lack strength. "Dropping the elbows" means relaxing the elbows downward and letting them hang. If the elbows are drawn up, then the shoulders will be unable to sink, and you will not be able to push an opponent far. Isn't this similar to the short energy of the external martial arts?

6. *Use consciousness, not strength.* This is spoken of in the "Taijiquan Classics." This is entirely the use of mind/intent (*yi*), not use of strength (*li*). In practicing *Taijiquan*, the entire body is loosened (*song*) and open; avoid the use of the slightest bit of crude force (*zhuo li*), which causes blockage in the sinews, bones, and blood vessels, and causes one to be bound up. Then you will enable a light agility in the changes, and the circular rotations will come freely. Some doubt: without using strength, how can one increase one's strength? Now, the human body has meridians—as with the Earth's watercourses, when the watercourses are unblocked, the water flows. When the meridians are unblocked, then the *qi* passes through. If the whole body is stiff, the *jin* fills the meridians, the *qi* and blood become stagnant, the turning motions are not nimble. If one hair is pulled, the whole body is moved. If one does not use strength but instead uses mind/intent (*yi*), then where the *yi* arrives, the *qi* then follows. If the *qi* and the blood flow fully, daily

threading and flowing through the entire body, there will be no time when there are blockages. After long practice, one then attains genuine internal strength. Hence, the statement in the "Taijiquan Classics": "Arriving at the extreme of of yielding softness, one afterward arrives at the extreme of solid hardness." The arms of those who are proficient in the skill of Taijiquan are like iron within cotton, and extremely heavy. When practitioners of external martial arts use strength, then their strength is evident. When not using strength, they are very light and floating. It is obvious that their strength remains as outward energy, as surface energy. When not using mind/intent (*yi*) but using strength, it is very easy to be led in—this is not worthy of respect.

7. *Upper and lower follow one another.* Upper and lower follow one another is what is referred to in the saying from the "Taijiquan Classic": "It is rooted in the feet, issued by the legs, governed by the waist, and expressed in the fingers. From the feet, to the legs, then to the waist, always there must be complete integration into one *qi*." With the movements of the hands, waist, and feet, the focus of the eyes also follows their movements. When it is like this, only then can it be called "upper and lower follow one another." If there is one part that does not move, then the form is scattered and confused.

8. *Internal and external are united.* What one trains in *Taijiquan* is the spirit, therefore it is said, "The spirit is the leader, the body follows its order." If one is able to raise the spirit of vitality, one will naturally be able to deport oneself lightly and with agility. The form is none other than empty, full, open, and closed. What is called open is not only the opening of the hands and feet—the mind/intent also opens with them accordingly. What is called closing is not only the closing of the hands and feet—the mind/intent also closes with them accordingly. When able to unite inner with outer as one *qi*, then there is complete continuity.

9. *Linked without breaks.* With practitioners of external martial arts, their strength is contrived and crude force (*hou tian zhi zhuo li*). Therefore it has its starts and stops, its duration and cessation. When its old strength is already depleted, its new strength has not yet been born. At these times it is most easily overcome. *Taijiquan* uses the mind/intent, not strength. From beginning to finish it is continuous without ceasing, a complete cycle back to the beginning, circling without end. In the original teachings it is said: "Like the Long River, it flows smoothly on without ceasing." It is also said, "Move the *jin* [energy] as though drawing silk [from a cocoon]." These words refer to its being threaded together (*guan chuan*) as one *qi*.

10. *Seek stillness in motion.* The external martial arts view leaping and stumbling as ability. They employ exertion of *qi* and strength, so that after training they are invariably gasping for breath. *Taijiquan* uses stillness to manage movement. Even when there is movement, there is stillness. Therefore, in practicing the form, the slower the better. When practicing slowly, the breathing deepens and lengthens, the *qi* sinks to the *dantian*. One avoids the harm of straining the blood circulation. Students should carefully contemplate this, so as to attain its meaning.

—Dictated by Yang Chengfu, recorded by Chen Weiming

Chapter Two

Yang Style
Taijiquan Illustrated

The Names and Order of Yang Style Taijiquan Postures

1. Preparatory Posture
2. Beginning Form *Commencement* Step
3. Grasp Sparrow's Tail *ward off, pull back, press, push*
4. Single Whip
5. Lift Hands Upward
6. White Crane Displays Wings *Stork Spreads*
7. Left Brush Knee Twist Step
8. Hands Strum Pipa *Play guitar*
9. Left and Right Brush Knee Twist Step
10. Hands Strum Pipa
11. Left Brush Knee Twist Step *Xu Chi*
12. Advance Step, Deflect, Parry, and Punch
13. Like Sealing, As If Closing *App. Close*
14. Cross Hands
15. Embrace Tiger, Return to Mountain *carry T to M*
16. Observe Fist Under Elbow
17. Left and Right Step Back Dispatch Monkey *Repulse 3X*
18. Flying Obliquely *Slanting*
19. Lift Hands Upward
20. White Crane Displays Wings *White Stork*
21. Left Brush Knee Twist
22. Needle at Sea Bottom
23. Fan Through Back
24. Turn Body and Strike *Turn & chop w/ Fist*
25. Advance Step, Deflect, Parry, and Punch
26. Step Up, Grasp Sparrow's Tail
27. Single Whip
28. Cloud Hands
29. Single Whip
30. High Pat on Horse
31. Left and Right Separate Feet
32. Turn Body and Kick with Heel
33. Left and Right Brush Knee Twist Step
34. Advance Step, Plant Punch
35. Turn Body and Strike
36. Advance Step, Deflect, Parry, and Punch
37. Right Kick with Heel
38. Left Hit Tiger
39. Right Hit Tiger
40. Turn Body, Right Kick with Heel

A Few Points of Explanation Regarding the Illustrations

1. Yang Style *Taijiquan* Illustrated has movement-analysis illustrations totaling 244, plus 7 additional illustrations, altogether 251. Among these, 76 are traced and drawn according to photos of Yang Chengfu taken during his life. The balance are in accord with the requirements and additionally drafted in the physical appearance of Yang Chengfu. Those that are traced according to the original photographs appear as follows, as a convenient reference for the student: 3, 6, 9, 11, 14, 17, 22, 24, 28, 33, 35, 37, 41, 43, 49, 53, 56, 60, 74, 78, 81, 82, 85 (side view), 87, 90, 92, 93, 96, 103, 105, 109, 111, 112, 115, 118, 121, 124 (side view), 127, 130, 133, 135, 139, 142, 143, 146, 153, 156, 160 (side view), 163 (side view), 169 (side view), 172, 175, 179, 181, 184, 187, 189, 195, 199, 202, 206, 207, 209, 212, 214, 217, 218, 220, 223, 227, 228, 230, 232, 238, 241, and 244.

2. In order to enable the reader to verify the directions of the postures, the postures in the illustrations have been appointed directions as follows: when the face is toward the reader, it is facing south. When the back is toward the reader, it is equivalent to facing north. When the face is facing the reader's right side, it is equivalant to facing east. When the face is facing the reader's left side, it is equivalent to facing west. After the reader has reached proficiency in practice, he or she can choose at will the direction according to the shape of the practice site; one need not necessarily start by facing south in the preparation posture.

3. The arrows on the illustrations' solid and dotted lines indicate direction of the hand or foot movements; all of the arrows indicate the direction from a given figure's transition to the next figure. In cases where the movement is comparatively simple, it is then possible to use the text to explain [them], so the directional arrows are not drawn on those figures. One can consult the text along with the accompanying figure to reach an understanding.

4. Solid arrows indicate the directional tendencies of the right hand or foot, while dotted lines represent the directional tendencies of the left hand or foot.

5. In order to illustrate the spatial characteristics of the movements' directions, the arrows are drawn according to principles of perspective: The scale near the reader is wide and large, the scale far from the reader is narrow and small.

6. Since the footwork in Taijiquan is fairly meticulous, shadows have been sketched next to the feet to help distinguish and clarify the relationship of the foot to the surface of the ground. Observe the following:

 indicates the entire foot is in contact with the ground

 when there is no shadow next to the foot, it indicates the entire foot leaves the ground

 indicates the heel is in contact with the ground

 indicates the toes are in contact with the ground

Yang Style Taijiquan Illustrated

The First Posture: Preparatory Posture

Figure 1

The two feet are in an open stance to the left and right, spaced the width of one's shoulders, the toes pointing forward. The body is naturally straight, the two shoulders hanging down naturally. The eyes gaze forward evenly. (Figure 1)

Important Points

1. The requirements are: "an intangible energy draws up the top of the head," "the qi sinks to the *dantian*," "the coccyx is centered and upright," "contain the chest and raise the back." According with these important requirements, relax the entire body, until your body stands in centered alignment and tranquil ease, and incorporate these principles so that they permeate all of the movements of the entire form. These prerequisites apply as Important Points common to all the movements of Taijiquan. When practicing one must bear them in mind from moment to moment. They will not be reemphasized one-by-one in subsequent Important Points sections, but only as needed to remind when there may be certain requirements that might easily be disregarded by the student. For example, in the postures *ji* (press) and *an* (push) of the Grasp Sparrow's Tail sequence, beginning students are frequently liable to bend forward or lean backward. Because of this, it is appropriate to raise these matters in the Important Points for that sequence. As for the remaining common

important points, although they may not be specifically mentioned, they still must be attended to.

2. As the two arms hang down, the shoulder joints must be loosened (*fang song*). The fingers curve slightly in a natural way.

3. The spirit of vitality (*jingshen*) should be naturally elevated. The mind should be calm, without a trace of distracting thoughts.

4. The greater part of the Important Points for the Preparatory Posture apply to the movements of the entire form. That being the case, this posture is the foundation for all of the movements that follow. Beginning students must pay particular attention to this.

The Second Posture: Beginning Form

Movement One: Raise the two arms slowly and steadily toward the front until they reach a height even with the shoulders. The distance between the two hands is shoulder-width. The centers of both palms face down. (Figure 2)

Movement Two: The two elbows sink down and naturally lead the two hands slowly and steadily pushing down until they are near the thigh, the fingers still toward the front, centers of the palms still facing down. The eyes gaze forward evenly. (Figure 3)

Figure 2

Figure 3

Important Points

1. Before raising the two arms, one must carefully examine whether or not the Preparatory Posture conforms to the requirements, then start the Beginning Form. At this time, one's thinking should take the lead, and must one concentrate on the direction of each movement. This, precisely, is to accomplish what is called in "The Mental Elucidation of the Thirteen Postures": "First in the mind, then in the body." For example, when raising the two arms in this posture, one first needs to be conscious of how to raise, then follow the consciousness in slowly and steadily raising up. Even though it may be a repeated movement, or one that you do proficiently, one still must do it in this manner. Otherwise, the inner and outer movements easily become scattered and disordered.

2. When practicing Taijiquan, from the Beginning Form to the Closing Form, each of the movements requires that you "sink the shoulders and drop the elbows." (See the text "The Ten Essentials of Taijiquan Theory.") For instance, when raising the two arms and pushing down the two palms in this form, the shoulders should not rise up, have tension or exertion—they should be loose, open, and sinking down. When raising the arms forward, the two elbows must not extend straight, they must slightly bend and drop. When the two elbows sink down, leading the two palms in the downward push, "Drop the elbows" is no doubt a very obvious principle. However, even when the two palms have already pushed down to near the thighs, there is still the requirement to "drop the elbows." Beginning students frequently find this point difficult to comprehend and think that since the elbows already hang down, one cannot, after all, "drop" the elbows from below the two palms. In actuality, in this type of posture (and subsequent postures also share similar circumstances) one must understand the following with regard to "dropping the shoulders": precisely that the two elbows must bend slightly, causing the forearms to curve slightly toward the front. In that way, the points of the elbows appear as though forming a

perpendicular line with the ground, still attaining the requirement of "dropping the shoulders." If, however, the forearms also hang perpendicular, then the idea of "drop the elbows" will be lost.

3. One must seat the wrists. To seat the wrists means to allow the heels of the palm to sink down, and the joints of the fingers to very slightly rise up. One must not, however, exert strength in raising the fingers—it must be natural. In this way, one will be able to direct energy (*jin*) to thread to the heels of the palms. The fingers will also experience sensations. Only when one is able to seat the wrists will one be able to "move [*jin*] to the fingers."

4. In Taijiquan, from the Beginning Form to the Closing Form, it is necessary to have linkage among all of the forward and back movements; one must not stop or break up the movements. The requirement is for an even pace, continuous without breaking, with complete unity and coherence. For example, in the present form, when the two palms rise up to the height of the shoulders, then descend, there can be no instance of stopping between these actions. That is, as each movement reaches a fixed point (*dingdian*, or "the ending posture"), one must accomplish what is called "seems to stop, does not stop."

5. As to the use of the palm in practicing the form, the five fingers should unfold naturally, with no exertion in opening them. One must also avoid loose, curled fingers; the palm must present a slightly concave appearance.

The Third Posture: Grasp Sparrow's Tail

Part One—Left and Right Ward Off (*Peng*)

Movement One: The toes of the right foot move (*pie*) out 45 degrees. As the body turns accordingly, the center of gravity gradually moves to the right leg. The right leg is bent at the knee and slightly squatting; the left foot lifts up toward the right, passing by the ankle of the right foot. At the same time, the right palm, following the turning of the body, passes upward before the abdomen, "wiping" (*mo*) a small circle before the right chest, toward the right, toward the inside, then toward the left. The heart of the palm faces down. The left palm concurrently passes before the abdomen, following an arc, and arriving beneath the right palm—following in such a way that the arm turns out, causing the palm to turn and face the right palm directly—the two palms are now opposite one another as though holding a sphere. The right elbow sinks slightly, a bit lower than the wrist, and the two arms appear as curved arcs. The eyes follow the turning of the body, the gaze looking slightly in advance of the arrival point of the right arm, then looking directly at the right arm. (Figures 4–5)

Figure 4   Figure 5

Movement Two: The right leg continues to gradually lower into a squat; the left leg takes a large step toward the left front, first touching the heel to the ground, then following the gradual movement of the center of gravity toward the left leg. The complete foot plants solidly, the toes pointing slightly southwest. The left leg is bowed, the right leg pushes from the heel, becoming a left bow stance. Just as the left leg steps forward, the body turns toward the left. Just as the left heel touches the ground, the body then gradually completes the leftward turn. At the same time, the left elbow bends slightly, and using an arc to the left and upward, the left forearm wards off (*peng*). The left palm is at the height of the shoulders, the wrist slightly turned in, the palm facing obliquely up and to the right. The right palm is toward the front, then plucks (*cai*) to the right and down in an arc to the height of the thigh, the palm facing down, fingers forward, wrist settled, finger joints slightly turning upward. The eyes gaze evenly forward and must make a connection where the two palms separate to the left and right. (Figure 6) Movements one and two are Left *Peng*. Movement three is Right *Peng*.

Movement Three: When the center of gravity has all gradually shifted to the left leg, the body turns slightly left, and the right foot passes by the inner ankle of the left foot, lifting upward and forward in an arc. While following the turning of the body, the left elbow withdraws slightly down, to the left rear, naturally leading the motion of the left palm downward to the left front of the chest. Following the motion, the arm **rotates** inward, causing the heart of the palm [the center of the palm] to gradually turn to face the lower right. At the same time, the right palm makes an arc to the left before the front of the chest. Following the motion, the arm **rotates** outward, causing the palm to turn and face toward the upper left, forming a ball-holding shape with the left palm. The gaze briefly attends to the withdrawal of the left arm, then gradually looks out in the direction in front of the right arm. (Figure 7)

Figure 6

Figure 7

Movement Four: The right foot takes a large step out to the right (west), first touching the ground with the heel. Following, the center of gravity gradually moves toward the right foot until it becomes a solid step, right leg bowed, left leg pushing from the heel, forming a right bow stance. At the same time, the body turns slightly right. Following the turning of the body, the right forearm concurrently wards off upwardly (*peng*) toward the right (west), the right palm at chest level, the elbow slightly lower than the palm. The left palm pushes forward, following the right arm. The eyes look forward evenly, and the gaze then attends to the right forearm's ward-off (*peng*). (Figures 8–9, and 9 front view.)

Figure 8   Figure 9

Figure 9, Front View

Note: Regarding the references in the movement narrative to the minute movements of **rotating** the arm out or **rotating** the arm in, an explanation is in order here. As for **rotating** the arm out, if you take the example of the right palm facing in (Figure B), then it is turning the thumb side toward the back of the hand or fist, causing the palm to turn outward, that is, causing the forearm's radius to separate from the ulna and **rotate out** (as if the arm in Figure B turned toward the outside, as in Figure A). **Rotating** the arm in,

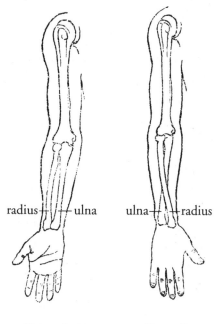

radius — ulna   ulna — radius

Figure A   Figure B

then, is the thumb side turning toward the palm of the hand or fist, causing the palm to face inward, that is, causing the radius to wind around the ulna, **rotating in** and crossing over the ulna (as if the arm in Figure A turned toward the inside, as in Figure B).

Important Points

1. When turning the body left and right, you must use the waist as axis. The body must remain vertically aligned. All of the subsequent turning movements of the body must be done in this manner.

2. The movement of the body, hands, and feet must be soft and gradual; the pace must be even.

3. Although the written description depicts movement of body, hands, and feet as having beginning and end, you must, however, coordinate them so that at the same time there is starting there is also completion. Therefore, in "The Mental Elucidation of the Thirteen Postures" it says: "Remember, when one part moves, all

parts move; when one part is still, all parts are still."

4. "The Mental Elucidation of the Thirteen Postures" requires that "When you step, move like a cat walking." Therefore, whenever you take a step you must always do so with lightness and agility. For example, take the form where the right foot steps out to the right—you must sit into the substantial left leg, gradually squatting down in order to control the right leg stepping forward steadily—only then can you avoid being clumsy and heavy. This is an expression of "clearly distinguishing empty and substantial" in the method of stepping.

5. When in the forward bow stance, the bowed leg cannot go beyond the toes of the foot. As for the foot of the treading rear leg, the entire sole and heel of the foot adhere to the ground, and the leg also must not be rigidly straight. In the bow stance, the bowed leg is substantial, the treading leg is empty. On the average, have the bowed leg bear 70% of the body's weight, the treading leg 30%. The knees and toes should point in the same direction.

6. When the right arm is warding off forward, it must be even with the shoulder; it can't incline high or low. When warding off, the shoulder joint should not protrude forward. Take as a standard the body moving forward vertically aligned, and yet with the knees covering but not going beyond the toes. At the same time, the body may not bend forward.

As the center of gravity moves forward, the leg, abdomen, chest, and hands must go forward together naturally—"not early, not late," "upper and lower follow each other." In the process of changing movements, one must observe "keeping the body centered and aligned" (*li shen zhong zheng*).

Part Two: Roll Back (*Lu*)

Movement One: The center of gravity gradually moves toward the left leg, as the body gradually turns left. Concurrently the left arm **rotates** out. The right arm **rotates** in, causing the right palm to turn and face the lower outside, while the left palm turns toward the upper inside. The two palms, following the turning, roll back (*lu*) to the left. (Figure 10)

Figure 10

Movement Two: The body continues its slight turn to the left. The center of gravity continues to move toward the left leg, sitting solidly over the left leg, making an empty right stance. The two arms, slightly sinking the elbows, follow the continuing turn of the body and roll back (*lu*) to the left. The left palm arrives in front of the right chest. As left roll back commences, the eyes at first attend to the right arm doing *lu*. When the *lu* posture is just reaching the point of completion, the gaze attends briefly to the left hand, then gradually turns to look toward the front (west). (Figures 11–12)

Figure 11

Figure 12

Important Points

1. In performing the left roll back, the arms must follow the waist, but the insides of the two upper arms also must not come too close to the ribs; sinking the shoulders starts an action that protects the flanks, but the armpits must retain a gap that would approximately contain a fist. All the movements of the form should be this way in order to avoid having your body restrained.

2. When performing the left roll back, the body must remain vertically aligned while turning; it may not bend forward, lean backward, or sway; the key point lies in "upper and lower follow each other," "not early, not late." If there is a case where the lower limbs sit back a bit too quickly, then there will be bending forward; if too slowly, then there will be leaning back.

3. In the process of doing the roll-back movement, because of the turning of the palms, sinking of the elbows, and the sitting back onto a solid left leg, etc., it appears as if the two palms are lowering. Actually, the two palms in no sense intentionally roll back "downward." This point also applies to the prescribed methods of *peng, lu, ji,* and *an,* the four postures of fixed-step push hands. Therein, roll back (*lu*), in like manner, is only performed toward the left (or right). There is definitely no downward action. Therefore, whenever there is a case of *lu* being done in a left- or right-downward direction, this is incorrect, for it will be out of conformance with the requirements of push hands.

4. During roll back, the left arm loosely holds the ward-off position (*song song peng zhu*). While in the process of rolling back, the two hands must maintain the same distance as they would in performing roll back in push hands, and they must be precisely consistent in having one hand adhere to an opponent's wrist joint, one hand adhering to their upper arm near the elbow, while drawing them in. Make the changes in distance between the two hands consistent with this, without drawing them too far apart. This is called "mutual interaction of the upper arms."

Part Three: Press Posture (*Ji*)

Movement: The body turns slightly to the right. At the same time, the body's weight gradually moves toward the right leg, the right leg bending at the knee, the left leg pushing from the heel, forming a right bow stance. Following the turning of the body, the right arm **rotates** out, causing the right palm to turn and face toward the inside. The left arm **rotates** in, causing the left palm to face toward the outside. The right arm appears as an arc shape laterally before the chest, the right elbow slightly lower than the right wrist. The left palm is on the inside of the right forearm. Using the right forearm and the left palm, press (*ji*) toward the right (west). The left palm, following the press, follows close to the "pulse gate" (*mai men*) of the right inside wrist. The eyes look forward evenly, the gaze attending to the right arm. (Figures 13–14)

Figure 13 Figure 14

Important Points

1. When performing press, the upper body must not bend forward or lean back. The shoulders must not rise up, but should be loosened (*fang song*) and sunk down. The buttocks must not protrude. The elbows must not lift up, but should be slightly lower than the wrists.

2. After issuing the press, the space between the left palm and the pulse gate of the right wrist should "seem near/not near."

Part Four: Push Posture (*An*)

Movement One: The left arm slightly rotates in, causing the palm to face down. The left palm passes over the upper side of the right palm—crossing palms, then passing. Following, the two palms then separate to a distance slightly narrower than shoulder width, both palms facing downward. The two elbows gradually bend, sinking downward, and lead the movement of the two palms wiping slightly downward and back. At the same time, the center of gravity gradually moves to the rear, sitting onto the solid left leg. The eyes look forward evenly, the gaze attending to the two palms wiping back. (Figures 15–16)

Figure 15 Figure 16

Movement Two: The two palms push toward the front, wrists at shoulder height. At the same time, the right leg bends at the knee, the left leg pushes from the heel, forming a right bow stance. The eyes gaze forward evenly, the gaze attending to the two palms pushing forward. (Figure 17)

Important Points

1. As the center of gravity shifts back, the right *kua gen* (thigh bone/

pelvic joint) pulls slightly toward the rear, allowing the body to face squarely forward, preventing it from slanting to the left corner.

2. The two palms wiping back should follow the *kua* (inside upper thighs and pelvis) as it sits back. Loosen the shoulders. Do not allow the elbows to stick out.

3. The two palms must follow the center of gravity shifting forward, then push out, manifesting a slightly upward curving arc. The degree of rise and fall, however, should not be great. The two arms and shoulders must not become tense or rise up. The elbows exert no strength in extending. The body must not bend forward or lean back.

4. When the palms have not yet pushed forth, the left palm is inclined to the right side; the right palm is inclined to the left side. As the hands push forth, the palms, following the push, turn toward the front. The two palms, however, must not turn to the point where they are facing squarely forward. Another requirement is for the heels of the palms to sink down, but with the thumb sides slightly raised toward the back.

Figure 17

5. When one begins to study *Taijiquan*, first one needs to be able to do the complete set of movements and postures with accuracy; then, in doing each movement, one must at the same time practice moving *jin*.

The energy points (*jindian*) of *Taijiquan* follow the movements and ceaselessly vary. Therefore the movements must be "continuous and unbroken" and "move as though drawing silk." Now, taking the components of Grasp Sparrow's Tail as our example, the following table indicates the locations and important features of their *jin*, as a convenient reference for the student to carefully consider and intuitively comprehend.

Moving *Jin*			
Figure Number	Right-hand *jin* point	Left-hand *jin* point	Principal part
4	In the wrist, on the ulna side	In the heel of the palm, on the little-finger side	Right hand
5	Shifts to the ulna	Shifts to the radius	Shifts to the left hand
6	Shifts to the little-finger side of the heel of the palm	Shifts to the radius, near the wrist	Left hand
7	As it lifts up, in the region of the index finger and thumb	While sinking the elbow, passes through the ulna to the heel of the palm near the little finger	Moves to the right hand
8	Shifts to the radius	Shifts to the heel of the palm	In the right hand
9	Shifts near the wrist in the radius	Heel of the palm	In the right hand
10	Shifts to the little-finger side of the wrist	Shifts to the area of the index finger and thumb	In the right hand
11	Shifts to near the wrist in the ulna	Shifts to near the wrist in the radius	In the right hand
12	Shifts to the little-finger side of the heel of the palm	Shifts to the area of the index finger and thumb	In the right hand
13	Shifts to the outside of the forearm	Shifts to the little-finger side of the heel of the palm	In both hands
14	Shifts to the wrist of the outside of the forearm	Shifts to the heel of the palm	In both hands
15	Shifts to the fingers	Shifts to the fingers	In both hands
16	Shifts to the little-finger side of the heel of the palm	Shifts to the little-finger side of the heel of the palm	In both hands
17	Shifts to the heel of the palm	Shifts to the heel of the palm	In both hands

Having discussed the *jin* points, we will now briefly discuss the source of *jin*.

The source of *jin* is: "It is rooted in the feet, issues through the legs, is governed by the waist, and is expressed through the fingers." (See "Taijiquan Treatise.") For example, in the transition from Figure 16 to 17 (in Push), the weight-bearing surface area of the two feet constitutes their root. For instance, if one is going to push a shopping cart, certainly one depends on the weight-bearing surfaces. If the two feet are floating in the air and have no weight-bearing contact, pushing the hand cart would be unthinkable. Hence the saying "it is rooted in the feet." (Practice includes weight-bearing surfaces in advancing steps, retreating steps, or *yuandi* standing postures.) With the right leg in a forward bow stance, the left leg treading to the rear, this is "issues through the legs." So if one pushes the hand cart forward, although both feet have weight-bearing surface area, certainly one must draw support from the front leg being bowed and the back leg treading to the rear.

When the center of gravity shifts from sitting on the back leg to the front, the waist very slightly rises, then lowers, coiling forward in an arc in order to guide the *jin* and control the movement in a forward direction. (Another example would be rotating the body using the waist in a turning movement left and right in order to guide the *jin* and control the direction of the movement.) This is called "governed by the waist" or "the waist is the axis." Passing through the spine and the muscles of the back; it is derived from gradually collecting and contracting, and turns by degrees into expanding; this gradually lets the *jin* coil and transmit through the shoulders, and elbows, then reach the heels of the palms in the forward *an* push. Moreover, the fingers also have the sensation of *jin* reaching them. This is called "the strength issues from the spine," then reaches "expression in the fingers."

At the same time, the turning transformations (*zhuan huan*) of *jin* must also be like this. For example, in changing from ward-off (*peng*) to the roll-back (*lu*) posture (Figures 9–11), while it also passes from the feet to the legs to the waist, one must take the *jin* point of the right hand in Figure 9, originally in the radius near the wrist, and move it to the wrist near the little finger, then let it reach the ulna near the wrist. Take the *jin* point of the left hand originally in the heel of the palm, move it so that it passes through the side near the index finger and thumb, and let it reach the radius near the wrist. However, there must not be in this process any sign of intermittence in the progression of movement from foot to leg to waist to spine; the movement must always be "successively threaded together" [*jie jie guan chuan,* from joint to joint], with "complete integration into one *qi*" [*wan zheng yi qi*]. Therefore it will remain true that "when one part moves there is no part that does not move; when one part is still, there is no part that is not still," that is, all parts coordinated. The chest and abdomen must also move in correspondence, under the driving power of the waist. By all means do not "contain the chest," and "loosen the *kua*" (inner thigh) as isolated actions, then be done with it without further heed, just leaving them in dull, fixed position with no movement.

Furthermore, the *jin* points indicated herein by no means imply using discrete muscle, employing strength, or tensing up. Rather the requirement remains that the muscular tissues be loosened, and that the movement be done slowly, gently, in accordance with the common Important Points. As for moving *jin*, it is also a matter of "first in the mind, then in the body." In using the consciousness to thread to a given position, the consciousness arrives, then the *jin* arrives—the place where the consciousness is concentrated will then have a resulting sensation. This is a case of the training method whereby "inner and outer are united."

If beginning students do not have an experienced instructor who can give personal guidance, they should just accurately complete the movements according to the Important Points. With the passing of time, owing to the accuracy and proficiency of the movements, the *jin* paths (*jin lu*) will naturally develop, and one will also naturally sense "upper and lower follow one another" and "inner and outer are united," and one will avoid developing deficiencies. Since each movement has fixed *jin* points and transitions, if we were to explain them one by one, there would be a tendency toward redundancy. Because of this, I have herein only provided an example by which the remainder may be inferred, and they will not be discussed one by one in the remainder of the book.

6. The saying "The eyes are the sprouts of the heart" means that from the eyes one can see the activity of the consciousness. This is just like actors' portrayals in theater or dance. When practicing *Taijiquan*, the expression of the eyes is an important feature in perfecting the form.

Let us try to raise an example in order to analyze the expression of the eyes. For instance, in the process of moving from left ward off to right ward off (Figures 6–9), as the body turns left, the left elbow withdraws toward the left rear and slightly downward, and the gaze connects with the left forearm (Figure 7); when the body turns right, just as the right arm is about to *peng* forward, the gaze shifts attention to the right forearm. (Figure 8) When the right arm has not yet concluded the *peng* move, the gaze is already slightly ahead, reaching the intended arrival point of the *peng* movement. (Between Figures 8 and 9) When the right arm *pengs* forward, although the eyes are already looking evenly forward, the expression must make a connection with the arm doing the *peng* movement. (Figure 9)

From this motion one can see and understand without difficulty that within the process of the movements, the eyes should integrate the idea of *zou gu you pan*—"looking both left and right." However, *zou gu you pan* is by no means to randomly look left and right without principle, but infers that the gaze must be in accord with the turning movements of the body. In actuality, with many of the turning movements of the body, if the eyes do not turn (the direction of the eyes and face of course being the same), the waist will also be unable to twist; then, in employing the kind of body turning required for a posture like left roll back (*lu*), the range of motion will not be great. But if the eyes still look in the direction of the ward off, although the body will still be able to turn to the left, it will be terribly awkward. Obviously, even if the body's range of motion in turning were a bit greater, there would still be no way to turn the body sufficiently.

In addition, when "looking both left and right," one must not neglect the requirement of the "intangible and lively energy at the top of the head"; one must not produce a wagging of the head when moving the vision left and right in a lively manner. Nor should one allow the head to incline up or down when the hand is doing an upward or downward movement, but must rotate the head as if "suspended from the crown" and use one's vision to attend. Only in this way can one actually express active agility (*linghuo*) and possess mental liveliness (*shen*).

As a movement approaches completion, the eyes must always move in the direction slightly in advance of the completed point of arrival of the hand, thereby manifesting "use the eyes to lead the hands," that is, the eyes must become the representatives of the mind, and as such, must integrate [the concept of] "first in the mind, then in the body." (See the preceding narrative.) For example, in daily life, when one has the idea of picking up an object, the eyes always look at the object first, then the hand follows and picks it up—the principles are the same. Therefore, whenever a movement is going in a set direction, the eyes should focus there first.

Although the eyes arrive first, this is certainly not to say that one may just disregard the movements of the hands without care. One must still attend to the movement of the hands until they have reached their destination. In this manner, one can coordinate all of the movements of the "hands, eyes, torso, methods, and steps," attaining the goal of "one part moves, no part does not move; one part is still, no part is not still."

The Fourth Posture: Single Whip

Movement One: The center of gravity gradually shifts to the left leg, the body turns to the left.* Concurrently, the toes of the right foot rise up slightly. Using the heel as the pivot, follow the turning of the body until the toes have turned in as far as possible, then plant the foot. The center of gravity, following, then shifts back to the right leg. At the same time, the two elbows sink and bend slightly, the two palms facing somewhat downward, answering and following the turning of the body, wiping in patterns of semi-elliptical planes. The palms are at shoulder height. The eyes, following the turning of the body, look evenly forward, slightly in advance of the left palm's destination to the left. The right palm, however, should be included in one's vision. (Figures 18–19)

| Figure 18 | Figure 19 |

---

*Translator's Note: Although the description of the transition from Push to Single Whip here and elsewhere in the text prescribes a shifting back of the weight onto the left leg prior to the turn, this differs from the traditional way of doing the movement in Yang Style Taijiquan. In the traditional form, one keeps the weight over the leg that is doing the pivoting. Fu Zhongwen's son, Master Fu Shengyuan *(continued on next page)*

Movement Two: The body turns slightly to the right; the two palms, following the turning of the body, wipe inward across the front of the chest and to the right in arcs, turning in semi-elliptical planes. The palms are at shoulder height. The eyes, following the turning of the body, gaze evenly forward, with the attention on the right hand. (Figure 20)

Figure 20

---

confirmed in conversation with me that his father did keep his weight over the pivoting leg in this movement. In Master Fu Shengyuan's English book, he notes the importance of weight-bearing pivots: "Rocking the weight back and turning with the empty leg will not develop the strength of the legs to the same degree as pivoting with the weight in the solid leg." Therefore, "If the original meaning of Tai Chi as a martial art is to be restored, then you must pivot on heel with the weight still in the solid leg." In order to do the weighted pivots correctly, "When practicing, keep the waist, abdomen, hip, buttocks, and groin relaxed while pivoting with the weight in the solid leg. As you are pivoting on the heel, the ball of the foot should be slightly raised. This is what is known as distinguishing the solid and empty in the foot." (Fu Shengyuan, *Authentic Yang Family Tai Chi: Step by Step Instruction,* (Victoria Park: Fu Sheng Yuan International Tai Chi Academy, 1995), p. 44.

Movement Three: The center of gravity shifts completely to the right leg. The left foot lifts up toward the inside. At the same time, the body turns to the right. Following the shifting of the center to the right, the right fist gradually extends to the right. As it extends, the five fingers hang down, gathering together to form a hook hand. As the body gradually turns left, the left palm moves upward to the left in an arc—as it shifts, the arm **rotates out** causing the palm to gradually face in. The vision attends to the left palm as it moves leftward. (Figure 21)

Movement Four: The body continues gradually turning to the left, the left foot steps out to the left. After one touches the ground with the heel, the center of gravity gradually shifts to the left, to the point where the entire foot is solidly planted. The left leg is bowed, the right leg extends from the heel, forming a left bow stance. Concurrently, the right hook hand continues extending to the right, with the shoulder loosened. The left hand passes in front of the face (at a distance of about a foot), moving toward the left. Following the move to the left, the arm **rotates in**, causing the palm to turn and face toward the front; then slightly push forward toward the left. The eyes shift evenly to the left, slightly in advance of the left palm's destination, yet the vision should attend to the left palm pushing to the left. (Figure 22)

Figure 21

Figure 22

Important Points

1. In Figures 18, 19, and 20, while the two palms wipe forward and backward, turning in elliptical planes, they must follow the turning of the waist. The two elbows, at the same time (with elbow joints sinking down), must also proportionately follow the wiping turns, bending and extending accordingly. As the two arms are turning, the distance between them should be constant; whenever the advancing arm goes, the trailing arm follows. "The two arms are mutually linked," not careless and sloppy. When the two palms wipe in, turning and passing in front of the chest, one must contain the chest and turn the waist, then the movements will be round and lively. However, in containing the chest one must be mindful of not letting the chest be concave, and also must pay attention that the chest not be stiff. Therefore the theory of boxing ["The Mental Elucidation of the Thirteen Postures"] says: "The intent (*yi*) and the *qi* must exchange with skillful sensitivity, then you will have a sense of roundness and liveliness."

2. The upper body is vertically aligned. Avoid leaning forward, bending backward, or slanting to the left.

3. One must "Sink the shoulders and drop the elbows" and loosen the waist and *kua*.

4. When in the fixed posture, the two arms and legs (left arm with left leg, right arm with right leg) must conform in direction— lower and upper must be perpendicular. Avoid the right arm slanting toward the right front; the knees must not extend beyond the toes. The tip of the nose, the focus of the eyes, and the fingers: all three points are focused together.

5. The wrist joints of the right hook hand should curve, letting the five digits gather together and drop down, forming a perpendicular line with the toes of the right foot.

The Fifth Posture: Lift Hands Upward

Movement One: The toes of the left foot turn in 45 degrees, then plant firmly. Sitting solidly on the left leg, the body gradually turns left; the right foot lifts up, settling before the left foot a step, touching the ground with the heel. The toes lift up naturally and slightly. The right knee is slightly bent, forming a right empty stance. While turning the body, the right hand remains a hook, then changes to a palm, separating with the left palm, elbows dropping from the left and right. The hands simultaneously gather toward the front, the right palm in front at shoulder height, palm facing left; the left palm to the back at chest height, the palm facing right, directly opposite the right elbow joint. The gaze passes through the right palm, to look evenly forward. This completes the lift-hand posture. (Figures 23–24)

Figure 23

Figure 24

Movement Two: The waist turns slightly to the left; the root of the left *kua* [*kua gen*, i.e., where the head of the femur joins the pelvis] draws in slightly. The right foot lifts up, while at the same time the left elbow eases toward the left rear; simultaneously the arm **rotates** in, causing the palm to turn downward. The right palm, also at the same time, follows the turning of the body from the front, then downward toward the left front, moving in an arc until it is beneath the left palm. Following the movement, the arm **rotates** out, causing the palm to face upward. The gaze observes slightly the easing back of the left elbow, then turns to face evenly forward. (Figures 25–26)

Movement Three: The right foot advances forward and lowers down at its original position, first touching the ground with the heel. As the waist gradually turns right, the right toes, using the heel as axis, gradually turn in and plant solidly. The center of gravity gradually shifts completely to the right leg. The right leg is bent at the knee, settling into a solid stance. At the same time one is advancing the step and turning the waist, the right arm presses (*ji*) forth. Along with the press, the arm leads the shoulder into *kao* [shoulder stroke]. The left palm, close to the inside of the right forearm, presses (*ji*) forward. The eyes first follow the right arm's press forward, then gradually shift to observe the right palm. (Figure 27)

Figure 25   Figure 26   Figure 27

Important Points

1. The process from Single Whip to the movement of the two arms in Figure 24 is one of "closing *jin*" (*he jin*). The movements of feet and hands must be coordinated as one.

2. When doing the posture in Figure 24, the two shoulders, the waist, and the inner thighs (*kua*) must loosen (*song*), the buttocks must not stick out, the torso should be kept vertically aligned, and the chest should not face squarely forward. The heel touches the ground in an empty stance, the toes are raised slightly—do not lift them too much. The right knee is slightly bent and must not be rigidly straight. It is important to settle the wrists. The center of gravity must sit entirely over the left leg.

3. In the process beginning with Figure 24 and continuing through Figure 27, since the *kua gen* draws in, the left leg must continuously maintain the phenomenon of slightly squatting down. While pressing (*ji*) forward, one must include the intent of *kao* (shoulder stroke) but must not raise the shoulders. The torso should be vertically aligned, with no bowing forward.

The Sixth Posture: White Crane Displays Wings

Figure 28

The Movement: The left foot lifts up slightly, moving in front of the right foot (east), using the toe to touch the ground. The left knee is slightly bent; the body turns slightly toward the left. Concurrently, the right palm rises up and forward, and while rising **rotates** in, causing the palm to turn and face outward. The left palm, also at the same time, falls downward in an arc to the side of the left *kua*. The eyes make a slight connection with the rising right palm, then gaze evenly forward, with the focus including both palms. (Figure 28)

Important Points

1. The process from Lift Hands Upward to White Crane Displays Wings must have an upward momentum (*cha shang de qi shi*), but

the right leg must remain sitting downward. One must elongate the waist. In this way, one has a mutual pulling upward and downward—a sensation of lengthening of the body and limbs. However, one must pay attention not to allow the thorax to become rigid. The *jin* pulls up the top of the head, enabling the spirit of vitality to rise up. Sink the *qi* and settle the *kua*. The lower body is thereby stable. The left toes should touch the ground in an empty stance; one must not use them to support the body.

2. While forming White Crane Displays Wings, the two arms must assume arc shapes, they must not straighten rigidly; although the right palm is before and above the right temple, you must not raise the elbow or the shoulder, but must loosen the shoulders, sink the elbows, and settle the wrists. The body must maintain its vertical alignment, without leaning forward or backward. Do not thrust out the chest or allow the buttocks to protrude.

The Seventh Posture: Left Brush Knee Twist Step

Movement One: The waist turns slightly to the right, the right *kua gen* (inner thigh) draws in slightly. Following the turning of the waist, with the right shoulders loosened and the right elbow sinking down, guide the right palm with a natural ease through a downward falling arc (passing by the right side of the *kua*). As the arm falls in an arc, the arm **rotates** out, allowing the palm to gradually face upward; concurrently, the left palm also follows the turning of the waist from the lower left, toward the front and upward (at the height of the diaphragm), moving in an arc to the right. The eyes, following the turning of the body, gaze evenly forward. The vision must attend to the right palm. (Figures 29–30)

Figure 29   Figure 30

Movement Two: The left foot lifts up, the upper body continues slightly turning toward the right. Following the turning of the body, the right palm moves up in an arc toward the right corner. The left palm continues to fall in an arc to the right before the abdomen. The eyes attend to the right palm, then shift to watching the left palm. (Figure 31)

Figure 31

Movement Three: The left foot lowers down toward the front, first touching the ground with the heel, and as the center of gravity gradually shifts to the left leg, the entire foot plants solidly. At the same time, the body gradually turns left, bending the left leg, extending the right leg from the heel, forming a left bow stance. Concurrently, the left palm, following the turning of the body, passes before the left knee in a semi-circular shape, "brushing" to the side of the left thigh. The right palm, also following the rotation and shifting of the body's weight forward, continues past the right ear in an upward arc toward the front (east), pushing forth. The eyes attend to the left palm brushing past the knee, then gaze evenly forward. The vision also must attend to the right palm's forward advance. (Figures 32–33)

Figure 32   Figure 33

Important Points

1. The movements of the two hands must follow the turning movement of the waist; when the waist changes from turning right to turning left, there should be absolutely no unsteadiness. Any leaning to the side, slanting, leaning back, or stooping forward would be inconsistent with the requirement of "keeping the body in vertical alignment." When stepping forward, the upper body must maintain its verticality; avoiding bending forward or leaning back. During the process of stepping forward, because one only has the support of the squatting leg, there frequently may be a tendency

to let the buttocks stick out in order to maintain the body's balance—this does not accord with the requirements of "contain the buttocks" or "keep the coccyx (*weilu*) vertically aligned." You must pay attention to these points. When one reaches the fixed posture, the two hands should both arrive at the same time; there cannot be a case of one hand already stopping and the other still in the midst of movement.

2. In the process depicted in Figure 30 to Figure 31, the right palm's movement from below toward the upper right must correspond with the lifting up of the left leg. As the body turns left, the change to a bow stance must correspond with the pushing forth of the right palm. All of the movements of Brush Knee Twist Step must be done in harmony, rounded and full, softly and gently. Avoid any faltering or angularity.

3. As the right arm relaxes and sinks down to the right, you must not allow a phenomenon of the right shoulder being lower than the left shoulder. The shoulders should be at equal height throughout the entire set.

4. In all cases of Brush Knee Twist Step, the arm brushing the knee should be arc-shaped; avoid extending it straight. The right palm pushing forward must slightly rotate as it pushes out. However, as it reaches the fixed posture, the palm should not face squarely forward, but must face obliquely, slightly to the left. Both the wrists should be seated.

The Eighth Posture: Hands Strum Pipa

The Movement: The center of gravity gradually shifts completely to the left leg. (As in the preceding narrative, the foot of the front leg in a bow stance bears about seventy percent of the weight—it should be completely settled and solid.) The right foot lifts up slightly and lowers down about a foot in front of its original position. The center of gravity gradually shifts completely to the right leg. The body gradually turns to the right; the left foot lifts up slightly and lowers down about a foot in front of its original position. Touch the heel of the foot to the ground. The toes lift up slightly, and the knee is slightly bent, forming a left empty step. At the same time, the left palm, following the turning of the body, rises up and forward in an arc. As it rises, the arm **rotates** slightly out, causing the palm to face toward the right, with the index finger at shoulder height. The right palm also at the same time, follows the turning of the body, withdrawing back and downward, the arm **rotating** slightly out, causing the palm to face to the left, closing in near the inside of the left elbow. The distance between the two palms, front and back, is such that it resembles holding a lute (*pipa*). The eyes look evenly forward, past the left palm. (Figures 34–35)

Figure 34

Figure 35

Important Points

1. In making the transition from Brush Knee Twist Step to Hands Strum Pipa, the shifting of the center of gravity forward and sitting back both require that the upper body be vertically aligned. You must not bend forward or lean backward.

2. When the right palm withdraws back, you must use the waist as the axis, loosen the shoulders, drop the elbows, and seat the

wrists. In this manner, with each joint threading together and collecting back, one uses the torso to lead the hands. One cannot first pull the hand back without regard to the shoulders and elbow.

3. When raising the left palm up, it must make an arc; the left arm should not extend straight.

4. When performing the movements of Hands Strum Pipa, one must have an inward momentum of sinking down, but one's spirit must still possess the idea of nimble dexterity and liveliness.

5. The requirements are the same as in point number two for Lift Hands Upward, but left and right are reversed.

The Ninth Posture:
Left and Right Brush Knee Twist Step

Figure 36

Part One: Left Brush Knee Twist Step

Movement One: The waist turns slightly to the right, the right *kua gen* slightly gathering in. Following the turning of the waist, the right shoulder loosens and sinks. The right elbow sinks down, naturally guiding the movement of the right palm in a downward arc, falling past the right pelvis (*kua*). While falling down thus, the arm **rotates** out, causing the palm to gradually face up. At the same time, the left palm also follows the turning of the waist, moving downward in an arc from the front to the right. The arm **rotates** in as it moves, causing the palm to turn face down. The eyes, following the turning of the waist, gaze evenly forward. The vision must include the right palm. (Figure 36)

Movements Two and *Three:* The requirements are the same as for movements two and three in the preceding Left Brush Knee Twist

Figure 37

Step. (See Figures 31–32, then Figure 37)

Important Points

Refer to the Important Points for the preceding Brush Knee Twist Step.

Part Two: Right Brush Knee Twist Step

Movement One: Using the heel of the left foot as the axis, turn (*pie*) the left toes out at a 45-degree angle. The body gradually turns to the left. Following the turning of the body, the left palm moves left and back in an arc; simultaneously the arm **rotates** out, causing the palm to face up. At the same time, the right palm, also following the turning of the body, moves from the front in a downward arc to the left. Simultaneously the arm **rotates** in, causing the palm to face down. The eyes follow the turning of the body, gazing forward evenly. The vision must attend to the left palm. (Figure 38)

Movement Two: The center of gravity gradually shifts entirely to the left leg. The right foot lifts up and steps forward. The body continues slightly turning to the left. Following the turning of the body, the left palm moves up in an arc toward the left corner. The right palm continues falling in an arc

Figure 38

to the left before the abdomen. The gaze includes the left palm, then shifts attention to the right palm. (Figure 39)

Figure 39

Movement Three: The right foot advances forward and lowers down, first with the heel touching the ground. Following, the center of gravity gradually shifts to the right leg, until the entire foot is treading solidly. The body concurrently turns gradually right, bending the right leg, pushing from the heel of the left leg, forming a right bow stance. At the same time, the right palm, following the turning of the body, passes downward before the right knee and brushes in a semi-circular shape to the side of the right pelvis. The left palm, also in accordance with the forward shifting of the center of gravity and the body's leftward turning, continues upward in an arc, passing by the left ear, and pushes forward (east). The eyes first attend to the right palm brushing past the knee, then evenly toward the front. The gaze should also include the left palm's forward push. (Figures 40–41)

Figure 40

Figure 41

Part Three: Left Brush Knee Twist Step

The movement is the same as above, only left and right are reversed. (See Figure 42, continuing with Figures 31–33.)

Figure 42

Important Points

1. Review the previous Important Points for Brush Knee Twist Step.

2. When practicing these forms, and the stances of bow stance and empty stance, the two feet must not stand on a straight horizontal line like this:

Standing in this manner, one will easily develop an unstable and awkward center of gravity. Rather, one must stand with the back foot and front foot both slightly apart from the horizontal line. A left bow stance should be like this:

A right empty stance should be like this:

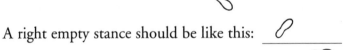

Therefore, in each instance of taking a step or retreating a step, one must pay attention that the positioning of the footsteps open out from this line a bit. Only then can you achieve stability. There is a phrase from the "Taijiquan Classic": "In advancing forward and retreating back, you will then be able to seize the opportunity and the strategic advantage." This sentence embraces the correct model and method of one's stance.

The Tenth Posture: Hands Strum Pipa

The movements and Important Points are all the same as for the Eighth Posture, Hands Strum Pipa. (Figures 34–35)

The Eleventh Posture: Left Brush Knee Twist Step

The movements and Important Points are all the same as for the previous Left Brush Knee Twist Step of the Ninth Posture. (Figure 36, continuing with Figures 31–32, and on to Figure 43)

Figure 43

The Twelfth Posture:
Advance Step, Deflect, Parry, and Punch

Movement One: The toes of the left foot turn out 45 degrees. The body gradually turns left, with the center of gravity immediately shifting forward to the left leg. The heel of the right foot leaves the ground (preparing to take a step). Following the turning of the body, the right palm moves toward the lower left (to the height of the pelvis), while moving, changing to a fist, and also with the arm

rotating in, causing the heart of the fist to face down. The left palm, also following the turning of the body, moves to the left rear. The gaze attends to the downward movement of the right hand, but the head must not be lowered. (Figure 44)

Movement Two: The center of gravity gradually shifts entirely to the left leg. The right foot lifts up and forward. At the same time, the right fist circles from the right front to the left and down; the left palm arcs toward the left and up, no higher than the ear. As it arcs, the arm **rotates** in, causing the heart of the palm to turn and face toward the right and down. The eyes attend first to the right fist circling left and down, then gradually turn right, looking evenly. (Figure 45. See Figure 99 for opposite view.)

Figure 44   Figure 45

Movement Three: The right foot steps forth obliquely toward the right front (southeast), first letting the heel touch the ground. Then the toes turn out, planting the foot solidly, and the center of gravity gradually shifts completely to the right leg. The left leg rises up, with the body concurrently turning right. Following the turning of the body, the right fist deflects (*ban*) out from the left, then up, passing before the chest; as it deflects, the arm **rotates** out, causing the heart of the fist to gradually turn to face in and up, then following to arc downward and pull back. The left palm, also at the same time, follows the turning of the body and parries (*lan*) in an arc to the right, passing by the inside of the right arm, with the heart of the palm facing right. The gaze attends to the left palm's forward parry. (Figures 46–47. See also Figures 100–101.)

Figure 46

Figure 47

Movement Four: The left foot takes a step forward, first touching the ground with the heel. At the same time, the body continues turning right. Following the turning of the body, the left palm continues extending forward, while the right fist pulls back in an arc to the side of the waist, the heart of the fist facing up. The eyes look evenly forward; the gaze must include the palm extending forth. (Figure 48. See Figure 102 for opposite view.)

Figure 48

Movement Five: Next, the center of gravity gradually shifts to the left leg, with the left foot gradually becoming solid. Bend the left leg, and push from the right heel, forming a left bow stance. At the same time, the body gradually turns left. Following the turning of the body, the right fist strikes forth, the tiger's mouth (*hu kou*) slowly turning to face upward. The left palm pulls in, seating the wrist, the fingers obliquely up and forward, in close proximity to the inside of the right forearm. The eyes gaze evenly forward. The vision should include the right fist striking forward. (Figure 49. See Figure 103 for opposite view.)

Figure 49

Important Points

1. While continuously advancing forward, one must remember: "When advancing, move like a cat." It is also required that one's pace be even, and that upper and lower follow one another. The upper body should be vertically aligned, not slanted, leaning, or stooping. When the right foot steps forward, it opens out more broadly than in most steps, but one must avoid letting the upper body follow the right foot and slant to the right.

2. Both stepping methods and hand methods should follow the turning motions of the waist. As the right fist moves forth in the deflecting motion, it must not be too far from the torso. Pay attention that the elbow doesn't rise up. As the right fist strikes forth, it must follow the turning of the waist, and while striking, the forearm **rotates** slightly in, causing the "tiger's mouth" to turn and face upwards. As the right fist is striking forth, it passes from the center of the torso forward. This is called "the fist issues from the heart."

3. When practicing the whole *quan* set, the fist should naturally clench solid; one must not apply strength and clench tightly.

The Thirteenth Posture: Like Sealing, As If Closing

Movement One: The right leg bends, and the center of gravity gradually shifts back to the right leg. At the same time, the left palm passes under the right elbow and extends to the right and outside, then strokes alongside of the length of the forearm. As it strokes forth, the arm **rotates** out, causing the palm to turn and face in. The right fist changes to a palm; sinking the elbow, pull it back in an inward-arcing motion. While deflecting, the arm **rotates** out, causing the palm to face in. The two palms are at shoulder height, the fingertips pointing up, and the two arms cross one another, the right on the inside. The vision includes both palms. (Figures 50–51)

Figure 50   Figure 51

Movement Two: The center of gravity continues to shift back, sitting solidly over the right leg. The two palms separate to the left and right, to a width somewhat narrower than the shoulders. While separating, the two arms **rotate** in, gradually causing the two palms to face one another. (Figure 52)

Movement Three: The center of gravity gradually shifts forward. Bend the left leg, push from the right leg, forming a left bow stance. At the same time, the two palms push forward. While pushing, the two arms continue to **rotate** in, causing the palms to turn obliquely toward the front. The wrists are at the height of the shoulders. The eyes look evenly forward; the gaze should include the two palms pushing forward. (Figure 53)

Figure 52   Figure 53

Important Points

1. As the body sits back, the two arms follow by collecting in. When the two arms cross one another, you must avoid any contracting or shrugging of the shoulders; you must loosen the shoulders and drop the elbows. The elbows are slightly separated. One must reserve some extra space beneath the armpits—about enough to contain a fist—but the shoulders must not protrude out or rise up. At the same time, the two elbows must not move to the rear of the body, which would put one in a difficult position.

2. As the center of gravity shifts back, sit solidly over the right leg as you loosen the waist and the *kua*. You must not allow a situation wherein the weight does not shift back, only to have the body lean back. In sitting back, one must maintain vertical alignment in the upper body. As the center of gravity shifts forward and retreats, pay attention that the chest and abdomen advance and retreat equally with neither leading nor trailing. Maintain central equilibrium in your body method with no leaning forward or backward.

3. Review Important Points one and two for the Push posture in the Grasp Sparrow's Tail sequence.

The Fourteenth Posture: Cross Hands

Movement One: The toes of the left foot pull in as the body turns left. Following the turning of the body, the two elbows bend into curves, separate, and open, bringing along the two palms, which move in front of the temples. (The distance from one's temples is about that of two fists.) As they move, the two arms **rotate** slightly in, causing the palms to face toward the front, and the two arms present a rounded shape. The eyes follow the turning of the body, looking evenly forward through the two palms. (Figure 54)

Figure 54

Movement Two: The center of gravity shifts completely to the left leg, with the heel of the right foot lifting first, then gradually the entire foot lifting upward and shifting to the left (to shoulder width). Then, with the toes touching the ground first, gradually plant the foot solidly. Then the center of gravity shifts to the right as the two legs gradually assume a standing posture, but with the knees remaining slightly bent, forming an open stance (*kai li bu*). Following the shifting of the weight to the left, the two palms separate to the left and right, then pass upward in arcs before the abdomen, crossing the arms in an embrace before the collarbones, the right hand on the outside. The point of intersection is about the distance of two and a half fists from one's collarbones. As the two palms pass before the abdomen in arcs, the arms **rotate** out, causing the palms to gradually turn and face inward. The eyes first attend to the sweep of the arms. As the palms are just about to intersect, look forward evenly. (Figures 55–56)

Figure 55   Figure 56

Important Points

1. As the toes of the left foot pull in and that foot becomes solid, then as the heel of the right foot gradually lifts up, it should resemble the rising and falling of a see-saw. This is also a kind of training method for making clear the empty and solid stances. When the right foot is solidly planted, a linkage is made with the next movement, then the toes of the left foot again turn in.

2. In each of the movements of Cross Hands, upper and lower must follow one another. As movements begin, movements are completed. Strive for coordination and consistency.

3. The two arms of Cross Hands assume a rounded shape. One must loosen the shoulders and sink the elbows; do not shrug the shoulders or lift the elbows.

4. When the two legs are straightening upward, every aspect of the body should loosen (*fang song*).

The Fifteenth Posture:
Embrace Tiger, Return to Mountain

Part One: Right Brush Knee Twist Step

Movement One: The toes of the left foot pull in, and the left foot plants solidly. The legs gradually bend at the knees and squat down while the center of gravity shifts to the left leg, and the right foot gradually lifts up, heel first. At the same time, the body turns to the right. Following the turning of the body, the left palm draws down from before the chest, then lifts in a leftward arc until it is at even height with the left shoulder, the palm facing up. The right elbow sinks down and naturally leads the downward movement of the right palm. As it moves, the arm **rotates** in, causing the palm to turn and face down. The eyes first watch the left palm lifting upward, then turn to look evenly toward the right. (Figures 57–58)

Figure 57

Figure 58

Movement Two: The right foot steps out obliquely to the right front (northwest), with the heel of the foot touching the ground first; then in accordance with the gradual shifting of the center to the right leg, the foot plants solidly. The right knee bends, the left leg pushes out from the heel, forming a right bow stance. As the body

69

continues to turn right, the right palm continues down, passing before the knee and brushing to the right side of the pelvis. The left palm moves from the left upward, passing the left ear and pushing forward with the turning of the body. The eyes watch the right palm brush the knee, then look forward evenly. The gaze should also include the left palm pushing forth. (Figures 59–60)

Figure 59   Figure 60

Important Points are the same as for the previous Brush Knee Twist Step postures.

Part Two: Roll Back

Movement One: The center of gravity gradually shifts to the left leg. At the same time, the left elbow sinks down, and the left arm **rotates** out, causing the palm to turn and face inward and upward. The right palm lifts in an arc from the side of the right *kua*, toward the front, passing by the inside of the left arm, in front of the left palm. The palm of the right hand faces down. (Figure 61)

Movement Two: The movements are the same as for movement two of Roll Back in Posture Three, Grasp Sparrow's Tail, only the direction is different. In the previous Grasp Sparrow's Tail, the bow and empty stances face due west. In this sequence, including the following Press and Push, the direction is facing obliquely to the northwest. (Figure 62)

Figure 61   Figure 62

Important Points are the same as those for Roll Back in the previous Grasp Sparrow's Tail (the Third Posture).

Part Three: Press and Push

The movements and Important Points are all the same as for Press and Push in the prior Grasp Sparrow's Tail sequence, except for the difference in direction. (Figures 63–67)

Figure 63   Figure 64

Figure 65   Figure 66

Figure 67

The Sixteenth Posture: Observe Fist Under Elbow

Movements One and *Two* are the same as those for the Fourth Posture, Single Whip, only the direction is different. (Figures 68–70)

Figure 68   Figure 69

Figure 70

Movement Three: The center of gravity shifts to the right leg. The body turns slightly to the left. The left foot lifts up toward the left rear (due east) and swings out. Following the turning of the body, the left palm moves in a horizontal arc to the left. While moving, the arm rotates out, causing the palm to turn and face in. Follow-

Figure 71

ing closely, the right palm, moves to the left in a horizontal arc. As it moves the arm **rotates** in, causing the palm to turn toward the front. The two elbows slightly sink and slightly bend, causing the two palms to mirror one another. The gaze attends to the left palm's move leftward. (Figure 71)

Movement Four: The left foot eases down to the left (east). The center of gravity gradually shifts entirely to the left leg. While the body continues to turn to the left, the right foot lifts up, shifts slightly forward, and eases down. The center of gravity then gradually shifts to the right leg. As the body turns, the two palms move in a horizontal arc to the left. When the left palm reaches the left side, it then shifts left and down in an arc. As the two arms move, they **rotate** in, causing the palms to turn and face down. The gaze first attends to the left palm moving left, then shifts to the right palm just as it moves in front of the chest. (Figures 72–73)

Movement Five: The center of gravity shifts entirely onto the right leg. The left leg lifts slightly, eases forward and left, and lowers down, using the heel to touch the ground. The body continues to turn slightly left. While the body turns, the left palm threads down roundly from the left, toward the inside, passing the inside of the right forearm and moving forward. The palm is facing right, the index finger at shoulder height, aligned with the point of the nose. The right palm "seals" downward [*gai*, as though stamping a document with a seal], forming a fist as it moves to the left, passing beneath the outer edge of the left palm and arriving below the left elbow. The eye of the fist faces up; the heart of the fist faces in. The eyes briefly attend to the leftward and downward coiling of the left palm. At the time that the left palm passes by the inside edge of the right arm and is just about to thread forth, the eyes look forward evenly. The gaze still attends to the left palm threading forward. (Figure 74)

| Figure 72 | Figure 73 | Figure 74 |

Important Points

1. The movements in the transition from Embrace Tiger, Return to Mountain to Observe Fist Under Elbow should be carried out in accordance with the requirement of "When one part moves there is no part that doesn't move; when one part is still, there is no part that is not still" and "continuous without stopping." Do not allow any angularity or stopping; you must do it with roundness, fullness, and coordination. The foot and hand methods should also follow the turning movement of the waist. The two feet should not be double-weighted, but should just rise and fall continuously, like a teeter-totter.

2. As the two palms are shifting evenly to the left, you must pay attention not to let the right palm swing down. In the process of shifting levelly, the right palm must have the wrist seated. The left hand leads, the right hand follows — the distance between the two hands remains constant.

3. Upon reaching the end posture in Figure 74, the left knee should naturally have a slight bend. Pay attention that the two

shoulders do not rise up, and that the waist and *kua* are loosened. The two arms must be rounded and not extend straight. The chest should not be facing squarely forward, but rather obliquely to the right front. The wrist of the left palm should be seated.

The Seventeenth Posture:
Left and Right Step Back Dispatch Monkey

Part One: Right Step Back Dispatch Monkey

Movement One: The body turns to the right, with the right *kua gen* drawing in. The toes of the left foot are still slightly lifted off the ground. At the same time, the left palm extends slightly forward. The right fist, changing to a palm, pulls back from beneath the left elbow and down in an arc past the abdomen to the right, arriving at the side of the pelvis. While pulling back, the arm **rotates** out, causing the palm to gradually turn and face up. The eyes attend to the left palm stretching forward. (Figure 75)

Movement Two: The center of gravity gradually shifts entirely to the right leg. The left foot lifts up, passing next to the inside ankle of the right foot. The body continues to turn slightly right. At the same time, the right palm, inclining slightly to the right, arcs up to shoulder height. The left arm **rotates** out, causing the palm to gradually turn up. The eyes attend to the right palm lifting to the rear. (Figure 76)

Movement Three: The left foot retreats back a step, the toes touching the ground first, then the whole foot planting solidly as the center of gravity gradually shifts to the left leg. The toes point northeast. The body gradually turns to the left; the toes of the right foot shift accordingly toward the front (east). Following the turning of the body, the left palm pulls back in an arc to the side of the left pelvis. The right palm pushes in an upward arc past the side of the right ear, and forward. The eyes follow the turning of the body as the gaze shifts forward levelly. The vision should include the forward push of the right palm. (Figures 77–78)

Figure 75

Figure 76

Figure 77

Figure 78

Figure 79

Part Two: Left Step Back Dispatch Monkey

The movements are the same as for movements two and three of the preceding Right Step Back Dispatch Monkey, only left and right are reversed. (Figures 79–81)

Figure 80   Figure 81

Figure 82

Part Three: Right Step Back Dispatch Monkey

The movements are the same as for movements two and three of the preceding Right Step Back Dispatch Monkey. (See Figures 76–77, continuing with Figure 82.)

Important Points

1. As you continuously link the retreating steps, you must pay attention not to tread on a straight line, but rather to open out a bit to either side. Just as one leg lifts up in preparation to retreat a step, the other supporting leg must not rise up in its stance; it must still preserve the height of the empty stance. Pay attention that the upper body does not lean forward.

2. As each palm pulls back, it must pass by the side of the pelvis. Beginning students often do this movement passing by the ribs, resulting in an angular rather than a curved shape in the arm. This then appears uncomfortable and awkward.

3. According to the above narrative there are three Step Back

Dispatch Monkey postures, that is, three retreating steps. In order to increase the range of the exercise one may also do five or seven. (It is necessary to end on an odd number in order to link up with the following posture.) However, if one does five or seven Step Back Dispatch Monkey postures, the following Cloud Hands postures must be increased correspondingly to five or seven. Otherwise, the Closing Posture will not end up in the original position.

The Eighteenth Posture: Flying Obliquely

Movement One: The center of gravity gradually moves completely to the left leg. The right foot lifts up and back. At the same time, the left palm arcs from the left upward and to the right; the bowed arm is placed in front of the chest, with the palm facing down, the hand even with the shoulders. The arm manifests an arc shape, and the elbow drops down. The right palm arcs down from the front, passing before the abdomen and to the left; the palm is facing upward, closing opposite the left palm as though in an embrace. The vision attends to the arcing of the left palm. (Figure 83)

Figure 83

Movement Two: The body turns to the right. At the same time, the right foot takes a step out toward the right rear (south-southwest).

First touch the ground with the heel, then, following the gradual shifting of the weight to the right leg, plant all of the weight solidly in the foot, bending the right leg, pushing from the left heel, forming a right bow stance. Following the turning of the body, the right palm using the thumb side splits (*lie*) forth to the right rear and upward, to the height of the temples. The left palm pulls down (or "plucks," *cai*) left and downward in an arc, to the height of the pelvis, with the palm facing down. The toes of the left foot turn in, following the splitting out of the right hand. The eyes, following the turning of the body, gaze evenly and shift with the turn. The vision includes the right palm splitting out. (Figures 84–85; see the supplemental side view of Figure 85)

Figure 84　　　　　　　　Figure 85

Figure 85, side view

Important Points

1. When the right foot steps out to the right rear, it is comparatively difficult to control the body's balance, and often when lowering the foot to the ground, one appears clumsy. One must sit solidly on the left leg, and loosen the waist and the *kua*, first turning the waist, and as the waist turns gradually stepping out to the right rear. Only then can you maintain a light agility. At the same time, you will avoid any forward leaning of the upper body.

2. As the two palms close in the embrace, the left arm must contain the intent of warding off (*peng*). When the right palm splits out to the right rear and upward, the energy (*jin*) rises from the feet, issues through the legs, is controlled by the waist, and flows through the spine. From the shoulder to the elbow, from the elbow to the hand, they are threaded together joint by joint (*jie jie guan chuan*) in the splitting movement. Body, hand, and steps are coordinated. When speaking of all parts arriving together, with nothing arriving early or late, one cannot have the hand split out in isolation, with no regard for the other parts of the body. One would then fail to attain the principle of "upper and lower follow one another," and the requirements of the *jin* path. Also, when splitting out, the right elbow should be slightly bent.

3. Since it is comparatively difficult to master the stepping out, one must also pay attention to the evenness of the speed in order to avoid the phenomenon of pausing or stopping.

The Nineteenth Posture: Lift Hands Upward

Movement One: The center of gravity moves completely to the right leg. The left foot rises up slightly and lowers down about a foot's distance forward from its original position. The center of gravity gradually shifts entirely to the left leg. The body turns slightly left. The right foot lifts up slightly and also lowers down about a foot's distance forward from its original position, with the heel touching the ground, the toes slightly raised, and the knee bent, forming a right empty stance. At the same time, the left palm arcs toward the front, moving up. The right palm, with the elbow sinking, collects in and closes up with the left palm in front of the chest. The right palm is in front, at the height of the chest, the palm facing right, aligned with the right elbow joint. The eyes focus evenly forward through the right palm. (Figures 86–87)

Figure 86

Figure 87

Movements Two and *Three* are the same as movements two and three of the Fifth Posture, Lift Hands Upward. (See Figures 25–27)

Important Points

1. In the process of moving from Flying Obliquely to Figure 87, the waist—along with the upper and lower limbs—must begin and end the movement at the same time.

2. The remaining Important Points are the same as those for the Fifth Posture, Lift Hands Upward.

The Twentieth Posture: White Crane Displays Wings

The movements and Important Points are all the same as for the Sixth Posture, White Crane Displays Wings. (See Figure 28.)

The Twenty-First Posture: Left Brush Knee Twist Step

The movements and Important Points are all the same as for the Seventh Posture, Left Brush Knee Twist Step. (See Figures 29–33.)

The Twenty-Second Posture: Needle at Sea Bottom

Movement One: The center of gravity gradually shifts entirely to the left leg. The right foot lifts up and lowers down about one foot's distance forward from its original position. The weight gradually all shifts to the right leg, and the left foot rises up. At the time when the center of gravity is shifting to the left leg, the right arm **rotates** out, causing the palm to turn and face left. The left palm follows the forward shift of the weight and swings slightly forward. Following the rearward shift of the weight and the turning of the body to the right, bend the right elbow. The right wrist lifts back toward the center. The left palm concurrently sinks the wrist. The vision attends to the right wrist lifting back. (Figures 88–89)

Figure 88   Figure 89

Movement Two: The left foot collects in a bit and lowers down with the toes lightly touching the ground, forming a left empty stance. The waist turns toward the left. Sit solidly on the right leg. The left *kua gen* draws in. Fold the waist and sink down. At the same time, the right palm, following the turning of the waist, pierces toward the front and down. The left palm arcs down and drops to the side of the pelvis. The eyes look forward; the vision must attend to the right palm piercing down. (Figure 90)

Figure 90

Important Points

1. When the left foot lifts up and collects in slightly to lower down, the right leg must squat down slightly. The toes of the left foot gradually lower down on an empty point of contact with the ground surface. The center of gravity must be completely supported by the right leg.

2. When the right wrist is lifting back toward the center, you must guard against shrugging the shoulder or raising the elbow.

3. When performing Needle at Sea Bottom, it seems as though the left palm has no clearly evident movement. Because of this, beginning students often simply neglect the movement of the left hand. In fact, the left palm should follow the forward shift of the center of gravity, the sitting back, the turning of the waist, and the advancing movement. Otherwise, it is not in accord with the requirements of "When one part moves, there is no part that does not move." Additionally, the two arms should not straighten but must be slightly bent.

4. The forward movement and downward piercing of the right palm must follow the downward squatting of the right leg and the folding of the waist. Moreover, you must use the shoulder to press the elbow, and the elbow to press the hand, piercing downward progressively through the joints.

5. When folding the waist, maintain a straight line in the spine from the cervical vertebrae to the lumbar vertebrae; do not lower the head or bend the back. The eyes observe the right palm ahead, but do not let the head rise up. You must pay attention to the energy

of the crown of the head and to the sinking of the *qi*—one *qi* threaded from top to bottom.

The Twenty-Third Movement: Fan Through Back

Movement One: The body turns right, straightening upward. The left foot lifts back. At the same time, the right palm lifts up from its position in front of the body. As it lifts, the arm **rotates** in, causing the palm to turn and face right. The left palm lifts up from beside the left pelvis and to the front of the chest, the palm facing right and the fingers pointing up. The vision attends to the right palm lifting up. (Figure 91)

Movement Two: The left foot takes a step forward, with the heel touching the ground first. Following the shifting of the center of gravity toward the left leg, it gradually arrives over the solidly planted foot. Bend the left leg, and push from the right heel, forming a left bow stance. At the same time, the right arm continues to gradually **rotate** in, bending the elbow, the right palm lifting in an arc and coming into place in front of the right temple, the palm facing out. The left palm edges along the right forearm and pushes levelly forward. The eyes look evenly to the left [east]; the vision should include the left palm pushing forward. (Figure 92)

Figure 91   Figure 92

Important Points

1. When the left foot steps forward, the right leg should be sitting solidly; it must not stand up. Do not be too hasty in setting the foot down; the rate of speed should be even. Also, guard against unsteadiness in the body, leaning forward, or inclining back.

2. The change to the left bow stance, the pushing forward of the left palm, and the lifting up of the right palm—all three of these movements must be done in unison.

3. In lifting the right palm, you must guard against shrugging the shoulder or raising the elbow. When the left palm pushes forth, the palm should not face squarely forward, and the wrist must be seated.

The Twenty-Fourth Posture: Turn Body and Strike

Movement One: The toes of the left foot turn in, the foot plants solidly. The body concurrently turns to the right. Following the turning of the body, the right palm arcs from the right, forward and down (forming a fist), and coming into place in front of the rib cage. The elbow is bent and the arm horizontal, with the heart of the fist facing down. The left palm arcs up, lifting to a point in front of the left temple. The vision briefly attends to the arcing motion of the right hand, then follows the turning of the body, shifting to gaze out evenly in the turn. (Figure 93)

Movement Two: The center of gravity shifts completely to the left leg. The right leg lifts up. The body continues turning right. At the same time, the left palm, following the turning of the body, arcs to the right and down, passing and dropping below

Figure 93

the outer edge of the right forearm. The
right fist strikes to the right front. The
eyes follow the turning of the body in an even
rotation. The vision should include the
movements of the two hands. (Figure 94)

Movement Three: The right foot lowers
down to the front (slightly to the right),
with the heel touching the ground first;
then, with the shift of the center of gravity
to the right leg, it becomes completely solid.
The right leg bends, the left leg pushes from
the heel. The toes of the left foot turn in

Figure 94

slightly, forming a right bow stance with the continued turning of
the body to the right. At the same time, the right fist continues to
follow the turning of the body, chopping forward and downward
in an arc, then drawing in to the side of the waist with the heart of
the fist facing up. The left palm concurrently draws back in an arc
to the front of the chest, passing the inside edge of the right forearm and pushing outward and upward toward the front. (Figures
95–96. For illustrations of the complete sequence of Turn Body
and Strike from the reverse side, refer to Figures 143–147. The movements of both sequences are exactly the same.)

Figure 95   Figure 96

Important Points

1. Both the hand methods and the footwork must follow the turning motion of the waist and must be coordinated as one.

2. When setting the right foot down, you must not plant it on a straight line [i.e., in a line with the rear foot]. Also, pay attention that the toes of the right foot point squarely forward, not obliquely turned out.

3. The process of movement in the form illustrated in Figure 93 should be manifested clearly and accurately; do not just randomly wave your arms. You also must not pause or stop in doing this.

The Twenty-Fifth Posture:
Advance Step, Deflect, Parry, and Punch

Movement One: The center of gravity gradually shifts back to the left leg, the body turning to the left. At the same time the left elbow, following the turning of the body, sinks down, and the left arm **rotates** out, allowing the palm to gradually turn to face up. The right fist, with the arm **rotating** in, extends forward and up to just above the left palm. The heart of the right fist is facing down. The vision attends to the right palm extending forward. (Figure 97)

Movement Two: The center of gravity continues to shift to the left leg, as the body continues to turn left. The two arms follow the leftward rotation of the body and roll back (*lu*). (Figure 98)

Movement Three: The center of gravity shifts entirely to the left leg. The right foot lifts back. At the same time, the right fist coils from the right, moves forward, passing down in front of the abdomen, and to the left. As it coils bit by bit to the left, the heart of the fist turns to face down. The left palm arcs to the left and up (no higher than the ear). As it arcs [upward], the arm **rotates** in, causing the palm to turn and face to the right and downward. The eyes briefly attend to the two hands coiling, then gradually shift toward the front in an even gaze. (Figure 99)

Figure 97   Figure 98   Figure 99

Movements Four, Five, and *Six* are the same as movements three, four, and five of the Twelfth Posture: Advance Step, Deflect, Parry, and Punch. Only the direction is different—this posture is advancing toward the west; the previous sequence advances to the east. (Figures 100–103. The reverse view can be seen in Figures 46–49. The entire Advance Step, Deflect, Parry, and Punch sequence may also be seen in reverse view in Figures 148–154.)

Figure 100   Figure 101

Figure 102   Figure 103

Important Points

1. This posture and the previous Advance Step, Deflect, Parry, and Punch sequence differ in the connecting movements leading up to it. The earlier Advance Step, Deflect, Parry, and Punch is preceded by Left Brush Knee Twist Step. This posture sequence, however, transitions from Turn Body and Strike. However, Figures 45–49 of the previous sequence and Figures 99–103 of the present sequence are the same.

2. Review the Important Points for the previous Advance Step, Deflect, Parry, and Punch.

The Twenty-Sixth Posture:
Step Up, Grasp Sparrow's Tail

Movement One: The toes of the left foot turn out, planting solidly. The center of gravity gradually shifts completely to the left leg. The right leg lifts up toward the front, with the body turning toward the left. Following the turning of the body, the left elbow relaxes to the left rear and sinks down, naturally leading the movement of the left palm, shifting it down to a position in front of the left chest. The right fist changes to a palm and moves in an arc from the front downward and to the left, arriving in front of the abdomen. While moving in the arc, the arm **rotates** out, causing the palm to turn and face left and up, forming a sphere-holding shape with the left hand, both arms held in arc shapes. The eyes briefly look at the left forearm, then turn toward the right arm and look evenly forward. (Figure 104, continuing with Figure 7)

The subsequent movements of Ward-Off, Roll-Back, Press, and Push are the same as in the Grasp Sparrow's Tail of the Third Posture. Namely, starting from Left and Right Ward Off (movement four), proceed to the end posture of Push. (Figures 8–17)

Important Points: Review the Important Points for the Third Posture, Grasp Sparrow's Tail.

Figure 104

The Twenty-Seventh Posture: Single Whip

The movements and Important Points are exactly the same as for the Fourth Posture, Single Whip. (Figures 18–21, continuing with Figure 105)

Figure 105

The Twenty-Eighth Posture: Cloud Hands

Movement One: The toes of the left foot turn in and plant solidly. The body turns slightly to the right. At the same time, the right hook hand changes to a palm, sweeping from the right and down in an arc. The left palm, following the turning of the body, shifts slightly forward and down, with the arm bending and the elbow sinking. The hand is level with the shoulder, the palm facing downward. The vision attends to the right palm moving downward. (Figures 106–107)

Figure 106   Figure 107

Movement Two: The center of gravity gradually shifts entirely to the left leg. The right foot lifts up toward the left (the heel leaves the ground first). The body turns slightly left. The right palm, following the turning of the body, moves in a turning arc from the right, down, and to the left, with the palm facing in. The left palm, also concurrently, moves out in an arc, leftward and up. As it moves, the arm **rotates** in, causing the palm to gradually turn and face down. At this time, the right palm also moves in close to the left wrist. The eyes follow the turning of the body, looking evenly forward.

The vision should make a connection with the right palm moving left. (Figure 108)

Movement Three: The right foot takes a half-step toward the left and lowers down, with the toes touching the ground first. Following this, the center of gravity gradually shifts to the right until the right foot is planted solidly. The body concurrently turns slightly to the right. The right palm, following the turning of the body, makes a circular orbit from the left, then up (to shoulder height) and to the right. The palm is still facing in. The left palm, also concurrently, moves from the left then down to the right. Following the movement, the arm **rotates** slightly out, causing the palm to gradually turn and face in (slightly slanted upward). The vision follows the turning of the body and observes the right palm moving to the right. (Figure 109)

Figure 108   Figure 109

Movement Four: The center of gravity shifts completely to the right leg. The left foot lifts up (the heel leaving the ground first). The body continues to turn slightly to the right. At the same time, the right palm follows the turning of the body, moving in an arc to the right and down. As it moves, the arm **rotates** in, causing the palm to gradually turn and face down. The left palm continues to move toward the right and up, approaching near the right wrist. The vision connects with the right palm moving right. (Figure 110)

Movement Five: The left foot steps laterally to the left a half-step, with the toes touching the ground first. Accordingly, the center of gravity gradually shifts leftward until the left foot is planted solidly. The body concurrently turns left. The left palm, following the turning of the body, continues to move from the right upward, passing before the face (at shoulder height) and to the left. The right palm continues to move in an arc from the left, then down. As it moves, the arm **rotates** slightly outward, causing the palm to gradually turn to face in (slanted, facing slightly up). The eyes follow the turning of the body and gaze evenly outward. The vision should connect with the left palm's leftward movement. (Figure 111)

Figure 110   Figure 111

Movement Six: The center of gravity gradually shifts entirely to the left leg. The right foot lifts up (with the heel leaving the ground first) toward the left. At the same time, the body turns slightly to the left. The right palm, following the turning of the body, continues to move in an arc from below, to the left and upward. The left palm continues to move in an arc from above, then left and downward. As it moves, the arm **rotates** in, causing the palm to gradually turn to face down. The vision attends to the left palm's move to the left. (Continues with Figure 108.)

Movements Seven, Eight, Nine, and *Ten* are repeated movement, the same as movements three, four, five, and six. (Figures 109–111, and continuing with Figure 108)

Movements Eleven, Twelve, Thirteen, and *Fourteen* are also repeated movements, the same as movements three, four, five, and six. (Figures 109–111, and continuing with Figure 108)

Movement Fifteen is like movement three. (Continuing with Figure 112)

Important Points

Figure 112

1. When moving the hands, the turning movements of the body must use the lumbar spine (*yao ji*) as the axis. You must rotate steadily and calmly. Do not casually wave the arms. The upper torso must not slant. Preserve the idea of "holding the body in vertical alignment."

2. The two arms must follow the rotational movement of the waist. This should be natural, full, and lively. When passing below, toward the left or right, and moving upward, the movement must contain the idea of sweeping upward. When orbiting above to the left or right, the elbows may not rise up. The forearm must be loosened and relaxed into the ward-off position (*song song peng zhu*) as it revolves. The two arms—one above, one below, one left, one right—alternate in rotation. When the left hand is primary, the right hand accords and follows; when the right hand is primary, the left hand accords and follows. Do not let the movement be loose and disorganized, or stiff and stagnant.

3. When lifting the foot up, the heel should leave the ground first. When planting it down, you must let the toes touch the ground first. As soon as the heel of the planted foot becomes solid, the heel of the other foot leaves the ground. There should be a continuous rising and falling, like the action of a see-saw.

4. The sequence from movement three through movement six constitutes one Cloud Hands. Afterwards there are two more that are repeated movements. Altogether, there are three Cloud Hands. As already mentioned in the above Important Points narrative for Step Back Dispatch Monkey, if the practice area is spacious and you wish to increase the measure of your exercise, and increase the repetitions of Step Back Dispatch Monkey to five or seven, then Cloud Hands must also be increased from three to five or seven. Afterwards, continue with movement fifteen (Figure 112), then continue with the following posture: Single Whip.

The Twenty-Ninth Posture: Single Whip

Movement One: The center of gravity gradually shifts entirely onto the right leg. The left foot rises up (with the heel leaving the ground first). The body continues to turn slightly to the right. At the same time, the right palm, following the turning of the body, moves to the right and downward in an arc. As it moves, the arm **rotates** in, causing the palm to gradually turn to face down. Still following, the five fingers drop down, collecting together to form a hook hand. The left palm continues its circuit right, then up, then left (drawing near the right wrist as it moves right). As it moves, the arm **rotates** out, causing the palm to turn and face in. The eyes briefly attend to the movement of the right palm, then shift the attention to the left palm. (Figures 113–114)

Movement Two is the same as movement four of the Fourth Posture, Single Whip. (Figure 115)

Important Points are the same as for the Fourth Posture, Single Whip.

96

Figure 113

Figure 114

Figure 115

Figure 116

The Thirtieth Posture: High Pat on Horse

Movement One: The center of gravity gradually shifts to the right leg. The toes of the left foot naturally lift up, following the rearward shift of the center of gravity. At the same time, the right hook hand changes to a palm. As the right elbow bends, the palm moves in an arc to just in front of the right shoulder. The left arm **rotates** out, causing the palm to gradually turn and face obliquely up. The vision attends to the turning of the left palm. (Figure 116)

Movement Two: The center of gravity shifts entirely to the right leg. The left foot lifts back, lowering down toward the inside a half-step, using the toes to touch the ground. At the same time, the right leg gradually stands up (the knee is still slightly bent). This becomes a high-form left empty stance. Following, the body gradually turns left. Following the turning of the body, the right palm shifts somewhat toward the left passing over the top of the left arm, and stretching forward in an arc. The fingers slant toward the left and forward. The palm faces down, at the height of the shoulder. The left palm passes under the right arm and draws back in a downward arc to just in front of the left waist. The left hand's fingers point obliquely to the right and forward; the palm faces up. The eyes look forward evenly. The vision should connect with the right palm stretching forth. (Figures 117–118)

Figure 117   Figure 118

Important Points

I. When the center of gravity shifts to the right leg (Figure 116), you must sit solidly on the right leg and must use the left *kua gen* [the pelvic joint] to gradually draw in and lead the movement of the left foot lifting up. At the same time, the upper body must not lean back. Just at the point when the left foot has left the ground and is drawing back, the right leg then gradually stands up. The energy at the crown of the head must possess the idea of rising up to the sky. Sink the *qi* to the lower abdomen. There is the intention of a mutual pulling up and down, an elongating of the torso and limbs.

2. The two arms must be shaped as curved bows. When the right palm stretches forward, the shoulders must not rise up. There must be a pulling up of the lumbar spine, but you must not thrust out the chest or bow the back. The right arm must not be straightened, nor should the fingers point forward. If the fingers point forward, you lose the meaning of "seating" the wrist.

The Thirty-First Posture: Left and Right Separate Feet

Part One: Right Separate Feet

Movement One: The center of gravity gradually shifts entirely to the right leg. The right leg gradually squats down. The left foot lifts up. The body, following, turns slightly to the right. At the same time, the right palm, following the turning of the body, wipes (*mo*) in an arc to the right and toward the inside. The left palm wipes to the left and forward. The vision attends to the right palm wiping right. (Figure 119)

Movement Two: The left foot takes a step obliquely to the left front (northeast), with the heel touching the ground first. Following, the body's weight gradually shifts toward the left leg, bending the left leg, pushing from the right heel, forming a left bow stance. The body continues to turn slightly right. At the same time, the left palm wipes, rotating in a large level semicircle from the left, then forward to the right, passing under the right arm toward the inside. The left arm is bent horizontally, forming an arc shape. The left palm is placed transversely before the right chest, beside the right elbow, the palm facing obliquely in and

Figure 119

up. The right palm wipes a large level semi-circle from the right, then in toward the left, passing above the left arm and toward the front, then stretches out obliquely toward the right front (southeast). The palm faces obliquely to the left front, and the fingers point obliquely up. The vision attends to the right palm's wiping orbit and outward extension. (Figures 120–121)

Figure 120   Figure 121

Movement Three: The center of gravity gradually moves entirely to the left leg. The right foot lifts up toward the front. The body, following, turns slightly to the left. At the same time, the left palm moves up slightly toward the front. The right palm folds in an arc from the right, then down to the outside of the left palm. As it folds, the arm **rotates** out, causing the palm to turn and face in. The two hands overlap, the left palm on the inside. The vision attends to the intersecting of the two palms. (Figure 122)

Movement Four: The left leg gradually stands up (the knee remains slightly bent). The right foot separates out obliquely to the right front (southeast) as the face of the foot naturally stretches out level, to the height of the pelvis. At the same time, the two palms separate and open to the left and right, the palms both turning to face out, the fingers facing up. The vision attends to the right foot separating out and also looks evenly past the right palm toward the right. (Figures 123–124. The supplementary Figure 124a is a profile illustration. This figure is drawn based on an original photograph of Yang Chengfu. Although this posture was not at that time photographed on the angle, but from the side, it is still included here. On the one hand, it allows the reader to see Yang Chengfu's original posture, and on the other hand it can serve as a reference for the side view. There follow in the text several figures added as supplementary illustrations for similar reasons, and these will need no further explanation.)

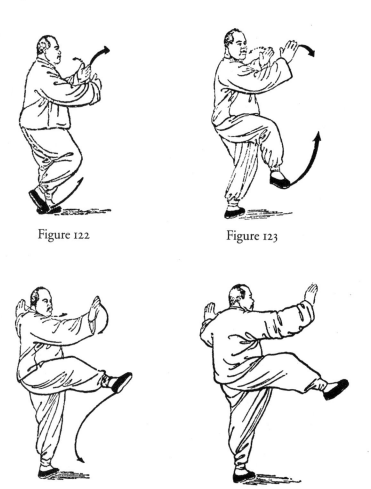

Figure 122   Figure 123

Figure 124   Figure 124a, profile

Important Points

1. When the two palms are wiping in semi-circular orbits, the arms must assume arc shapes. The elbows sink slightly. The wiping orbits should be even. When the right arm stretches out after its wiping orbit, it must not extend straight.

2. After the two palms close and overlap, they still must follow the motion of the left leg standing up, and gently move up and out; only then will there be an appearance of light agility and sunken stability. If the two crossed palms do not move when the left leg stands up, this can produce a dull and wooden appearance. When closing in the embrace, the two palms and wrists must not be slackened and curved.

3. The separating of the two hands must be unified with the separating of the right foot. Furthermore, the two arms must not extend straight but must bend slightly at the elbows, allowing the arms to curve slightly in front of the body. The elbows must also sink slightly—lower than the wrists—and the wrists must be seated.

4. The body should be stable when the foot separates, with no bending forward or back or inclining. The shoulders should not become tense in order to maintain the body's equilibrium; you must still loosen the shoulders. Only when there is the "light intangible energy at the crown of the head" and the "*qi* sinks to the *dantian*" can you maintain the body's balance.

Part Two: Left Separate Feet

Movement One: The right foot lowers down. The left leg gradually squats down while the body turns slightly to the right. At the same time, the left palm, with the arm bending at the elbow, wipes to the right. As it wipes, the arm **rotates** in, causing the palm to gradually turn and face down. The right palm wipes forward from the right. As it wipes, the arm **rotates** out, causing the palm to gradually turn and face up. (Figure 125)

Movements Two, Three, and *Four* are the same as movements two, three, and four for the preceding Right Separate Feet, only left and right are reversed. Right Separate Feet is toward the northeast; Left Separate Feet is toward the southeast. (Figures 126–130)

Figure 125   Figure 126   Figure 127

Figure 128   Figure 129   Figure 130

Important Points are the same as for Right Separate Feet, only left and right are reversed.

The Thirty-Second Posture:
Turn Body and Kick with Heel

Movement One: The left foot drops down, with the left knee slightly lifted. Using the right heel as the axis, the body swiftly turns to the left rear. At the same time, the two palms close, collect, and intersect in front of the chest, the left palm on the outside. The two palms face in. The eyes follow the turning of the body and look out evenly. (Figures 131–132)

Figure 131

Figure 132

Movement Two: The two palms separate and open to the left and right. At the same time, the left foot, using the heel, slowly kicks forth to the left, the toes pointing up. The right leg, with the left foot's kick, gradually stands up, with the right knee remaining slightly bent. The eyes attend to the left palm separating out and look evenly past the left palm to the left. (Figure 133)

Figure 133

Important Points

1. Review Important Points three and four for Right Separate Feet.

2. The left leg must follow the turning of the body and draw back in. It may not touch the ground. There must be the prerequisite of "contain the chest and pull up the back." Do not lean back.

3. When the left foot kicks out, you must use the heel as the forceful point of contact.

Note: When teacher Yang Chengfu originally performed Separate Feet and Kick with Heel, the motions were all performed with swift kicks after the lifting of the knee, with the energy (*jin*) expressing through to the toes or heel. When kicking, there was the sound of a burst of wind. Later, he revised the kicks to be done slowly and gradually.

The Thirty-Third Posture:
Left and Right Brush Knee Twist Step

Part One: Left Brush Knee Twist Step

Movement One: The left foot collects back. The right leg gradually squats down. At the same time, the left palm brushes in an arc to the right, passing in front of the left chest toward the left and down. The right palm moves in an arc to a point beside the right ear. As it moves, the arm **rotates** out and the elbow sinks, causing the palm to face obliquely toward one's head. The vision briefly attends to the left palm brushing downward, then turns toward the front [west]. (Figure 134)

Movement Two: The left foot lowers down to the front, with the heel touching the ground first. Following, the center of gravity gradually shifts to the left leg until the entire foot is

Figure 134

planted solidly. At the same time, the body gradually turns to the left, bending the left leg, pushing straight from the right heel, forming a left bow stance. Simultaneously, the left palm, following the turning of the body, brushes down past the front of the left knee, arriving beside the left *kua*. The right palm, also following the shift forward of the center of gravity and the turning left of the body, pushes out to the front (west). The eyes look forward evenly. The vision should connect with the right palm pushing forward. (Figure 135)

Figure 135

Part Two: Right Brush Knee Twist Step

The movements are identical to those of Right Brush Knee Twist Step, part two of the Ninth Posture, only the direction is reversed. The Ninth Posture progresses to the east; this posture faces west (Figures 136–139. For the reversed view, refer to Figures 38–41.)

Figure 136

Figure 137

Figure 138   Figure 139

Important Points are the same as those for the Ninth Posture, Left and Right Brush Knee Twist Step.

The Thirty-Fourth Posture: Advance Step, Plant Punch

Movement One: The toes of the right foot turn out and plant solidly. The body gradually turns right. The center of gravity, following, gradually shifts to the right leg. The left leg (with the heel leaving the ground first) lifts up toward the front. At the same time, the left palm, following the turning of the body, brushes in an arc from the front to the right and down. The right palm arcs from the right side of the *kua* to the right and back, then forward (changing to a fist). The vision attends to the left palm brushing down. (Figures 140–141)

Movement Two: The left foot takes a step out to the front, with the heel touching the ground first. Following, the center of gravity gradually shifts to the left leg until the entire foot is planted solidly. Bend the left leg, and push from the right heel, forming a left bow stance. The body concurrently turns gradually to the left. Sink the waist and the *kua* following the turning of the body. The left palm continues arcing down, then passes in front of the left knee to arrive beside the knee. The right fist strikes forward and down to a point lower than the knee. The eyes look forward. The vision should include the right fist striking downward. (Figure 142)

Figure 140   Figure 141

Important Points

1. At the point when the heel of the left foot stepping forward has still not touched the ground, pay attention that the upper body maintains its vertical alignment. When the left palm has brushed past the left knee, the upper body, following the downward strike of the right fist, folds at the waist and sinks the waist and *kua*.

Figure 142

However, when folding the waist, you must continue to maintain a straight line from the cervical vertebrae to the lumbar vertebrae. You must not bow the back or lower or raise the head.

2. The vision is in the direction of the right fist, but do not raise the head.

3. The two elbows must be slightly bent, not extended straight.

The Thirty-Fifth Posture: Turn Body and Strike

Movement One: The toes of the left foot turn in, then plant solidly. At the same time, the body straightens up, turning right. Following the turning of the body, the right fist, with the arm held horizontally and the elbow bent, shifts to a position in front of the left rib cage. The eyes follow the turning of the body and look out evenly. The vision should include the movements of the two hands. (Figure 143)

Figure 143

Movements Two and *Three* are the same as movements two and three for the Twenty-Fourth posture, Turn Body and Strike, only the direction is reversed. (Figures 144–146. For the reverse view, refer to Figures 94–96.)

Figure 144   Figure 145   Figure 146

Important Points: Review the Important Points for the Twenty-Fourth Posture, Turn Body and Strike.

The Thirty-Sixth Posture:
Advance Step, Deflect, Parry, and Punch

The movements and Important Points are all the same as for the Twenty-Fifth Posture: Advance Step Deflect, Parry, and Punch, only the direction is reversed. (Figures 147–153. For the reverse view, refer to Figures 97–103.)

Figure 147　　　　　　　　Figure 148

Figure 149　　　　Figure 150　　　　Figure 151

Figure 152   Figure 153

The Thirty-Seventh Posture: Right Kick with Heel

Movement One: The toes of the left foot turn out, planting solidly. The body gradually turns left to sit solidly over the left leg. The center of gravity gradually moves entirely to the left leg. The right foot lifts up toward the front (with the heel leaving the ground first). At the same time, the left palm, following the turning of the body, moves upward toward the left front. As it moves, the arm **rotates** out, causing the palm to turn to face in. The right fist changes to a palm and moves in an arc from the right front downward and to the left and up, closing in an embrace with the left palm, overlapping, with the right palm on the outside. As it moves, the arm **rotates** out, causing the palm to turn and face in. The eyes look evenly to the right front; the vision should include the two palms closing. (Figures 154–155)

Movement Two: The two palms separate open to the left and right. At the same time, the right foot slowly kicks out with the heel, the toes pointed up. The left leg, following with the kicking of the right heel, gradually stands up, but with the knee remaining slightly bent. The eyes attend to the right palm separating out, looking out evenly past the right palm. (Figure 156)

Figure 154

Figure 155

Important Points

1. Review Important Points three and four for the Thirty-First Posture, Left and Right Separate Feet.

2. When the right foot kicks out, the heel of the foot is the focal point of force.

Figure 156

The Thirty-Eighth Posture: Left Hit Tiger

Movement One: The right foot drops down. The left leg gradually squats down. The left palm moves levelly in an arc from the left toward the front and right. As it shifts, the arm **rotates** out, causing the palm to gradually turn and face in. The right palm concurrently shifts slightly down. As it shifts, the arm **rotates** in, causing the palm to gradually turn and face down. The vision attends to the right palm. (Figure 157)

Movement Two: The right foot drops down to arrive beside the left foot. The distance between the two feet is slightly narrower than shoulder-width. Step down with the toes touching the ground first. Following, the center of gravity gradually shifts to the right foot, and the entire foot plants solidly. The left foot thereupon lifts up (with the heel leaving the ground first). The two palms, following the shift of the weight to the right leg, continue to move to the right and down. The left palm passes in front of the right upper arm; as it moves, the left arm continues its outward rotation, causing the palm to turn and face up. The eyes look forward evenly. The vision should include the two palms. (Figure 158)

Figure 157

Figure 158

Movement Three: The left foot takes an oblique step out toward the left rear (west-northwest), with the heel touching the ground first. Following, the center of gravity shifts to the left leg, then the complete foot plants solidly. Bend the left leg, and push from the right heel, forming a left bow stance. The body concurrently turns left. Following the shift of the weight to the left and the turning of the body, the left palm makes an arc from in front of the right upper arm, downward, toward the left, passing in front of the left knee (changing to a fist), then up, arriving above and in front of the left temple. As the left palm changes to a fist and arcs from the left upward, the arm **rotates** in, causing the palm to gradually turn and face out. The right palm changes to a fist and, following the turning of the body, moves leftward from the right, the elbow bent and the arm horizontal, to arrive in front of the chest. The heart of the fist faces in; the eye of the fist faces up. The two fists are vertically aligned with one another. The eyes first watch the left fist. When the left fist is about to arrive in front of the left temple, the eyes then shift to looking evenly forward. (Figures 159–160, and supplemental side and front views, 160a and b)

Figure 159

Figure 160

Figure 160a

Figure 160b

Important Points

1. After the right foot kicks with the heel and drops down, the left leg correspondingly squats down in order to control the light and gradual placement of the right foot on the ground. In this way, it completely accords with the requirements of light agility and sinking. If it is only the right foot lowering down independently, then it appears dull and wooden.

2. When the left foot steps out, you must pay attention to the requirement of "stepping like a cat moving." Moreover, maintain the vertical alignment of the upper body.

3. While the two arms are making the transition to the Hit Tiger posture, the arcs must be done roundly; there should be no angularity. The upper and lower limbs should follow one another in unity.

4. When the left hand passes in front of the left knee, the left palm facing up should have the intent of "Brush Knee."

5. When forming the Hit Tiger posture, the two arms must assume arc shapes, "storing up within the curved" (*quxu*) with rounded fullness. Prevent the shoulders from rising up.

The Thirty-Ninth Posture: Right Hit Tiger

Movement One: The toes of the left foot turn in, then plant solidly. The body gradually turns right, sitting solidly on the left leg. The right foot gradually lifts up, the heel leaving the floor first. At the same time, the left fist changes to a palm, arcs toward the left and drops downward, the palm facing down. The right fist changes to a palm, the arm **rotating** out, causing the palm to face up, and moves in front of the left upper arm. The eyes briefly attend to the left palm, then follow the turning of the body, gazing out. (Figure 161)

Movement Two: The center of gravity gradually shifts completely to the left leg. The body continues in its rightward turn. The right foot lifts up toward the center, then it takes an oblique step out to the right front (southeast), with the heel touching the ground first. Following, the center of gravity gradually shifts to the right leg until it is completely planted solid. Bend the right leg, push from the left heel, forming a right bow stance. Following the turning of the body and the shifting of the weight, the right palm arcs from in front of the left upper arm, downward to the right, passing in front of the right knee (changing into a fist) and up, arriving above and in front of the right temple. Just as the right palm changes to a fist, arcing upward from the right, the right arm **rotates** in, causing the palm to gradually turn and face out. The left palm, at the same time, changes into a fist and, following the turning of the body, moves forward and rightward from the left, the elbow bent and the arm horizontal, arriving in front of the chest. The heart of the fist faces in; the eye of the fist faces up. The two fists are vertically aligned with one another. The eyes first watch the right fist. When the right fist is about to arrive in front of the right temple, the eyes then shift to looking evenly forward. (Figures 162–163)

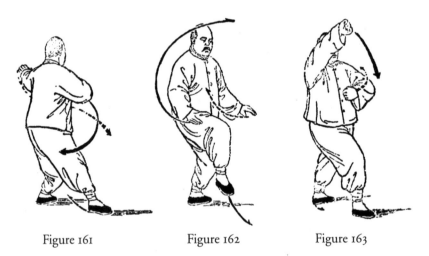

Figure 161   Figure 162   Figure 163

Important Points are the same as for Left Hit Tiger, only left and right are reversed.

Figure 163, profile

The Fortieth Posture: Turn Body, Kick with Right Heel

Movement One: The left foot uses the ball of the foot as an axis; the heel grinds (*nao*) inward and plants solidly. The body gradually turns to the left. The center of gravity, following, shifts leftward. At the same time, the left fist, following the turning of the body, moves levelly toward the left. The right fist moves in an arc to the right and down. (At this time, the two fists have already begun to relax open.) The eyes, following the turning of the body, look out evenly. (Figure 164)

Movement Two: The center of gravity gradually shifts entirely to the left leg. The body continues to turn slightly to the left. The right foot lifts and draws in. At the same time, the two fists change to palms, the left palm extending to the left, forward, and up, as the right palm is moving down, passing in front of the abdomen, then to the left to close in an overlapping embrace with the left palm. The left palm is on the inside. The palms

Figure 164

are both facing in. The eyes briefly attend to the left palm extending, then turn to look evenly forward. (Figure 165)

Movement Three is the same as movement two of the Thirty-Seventh Posture, Right Kick with Heel. (Figure 166)

Figure 165   Figure 166

Important Points: Review the Important Points for the previous Right Kick with Heel.

The Forty-First Posture: Twin Peaks Strike the Ears

Movement One: The right foot drops down, with the right knee still lifting up. Using the ball of the left foot as a pivot, the body swiftly turns 45 degrees to the right (obliquely toward the northeast). At the same time the two palms, following the turning of the body, both shift in arcs from left to right, arriving in front of the chest. As they shift, the elbows bend and the arms **rotate** out, causing the palms to turn and face inward and upward. The two elbows sink down, and the two arms assume arc shapes. The palms, from thumb to thumb, are shoulder-width apart. The eyes follow the turning of the body, looking forward levelly. The vision should include the closing of the two arms. (Figure 167)

Movement Two: The left leg gradually squats down. The right

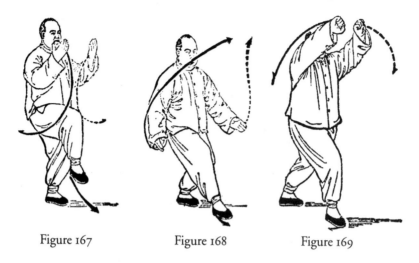

Figure 167   Figure 168   Figure 169

foot takes a step forward (southeast), with the heel touching the ground first. Following, the center of gravity shifts toward the right leg until the whole foot is planted solidly. Bend the right leg, push forward from the left heel, forming a right bow stance. At the same time, the two palms move down past either side of the right knee, separating left and right into arcs. As they separate, the two arms **rotate** in. Thereupon, the palms change to fists striking forward and upward, using the corners of the "tiger's mouth," forming a pincer-like shape. The two fists are at head height, the two "tiger's mouths" opposite one another. The eyes look forward levelly. The vision should include the two fists. (Figures 168–169, and 169a, front view)

Figure 169a, front view

Important Points

1. When you step out with the right foot, you must sit solidly on the left leg, draw in the right *kua gen*, then gradually squat down on the left leg in order to control the step with the right leg. Maintain vertical alignment in the upper body. The cadence of the

stepping forward must be even.

2. Following the lowering of the *kua*, the sinking of the *qi*, and the loosening of the shoulders, when the two palms pass down on either side of the knee, you must use the two elbows sinking down to lead the movement of the two palms falling down. It cannot merely be the two palms falling; you must use the energy (*jin*) of the entire body, causing the back of the palms to sink and loosen completely in dropping down.

3. The two fists striking forward and upward must be coordinated as one with the right bow stance.

The Forty-Second Posture: Left Kick with Heel

Movement One: The toes of the right foot turn out, planting solidly. The center of gravity gradually shifts completely to the right leg. The body turns slightly to the right. The left foot lifts up toward the front (with the heel leaving the ground first). At the same time, the two fists change to palms and separate left and right, then downward, passing in front of the abdomen in upward arcs, closing in an embrace, intersecting in front of the chest. The left palm is on the outside. As they arc, the two arms **rotate** out, causing the palms to gradually turn and face in. The eyes first observe the arcing of the two palms. Just as the two palms are about to intersect, the eyes then turn and look levelly toward the left. (Figures 170–171)

Movement Two: The two palms separate to the left and right. At the same time, the left foot slowly kicks to the left with the heel. The right leg, following with the kicking out of the left foot, gradually stands up, with the knee still slightly bent. The vision attends to the left palm separating open, then past the left palm to gaze evenly forward. (Figure 172)

Figure 170

Figure 171

Important Points: Review the Important Points for the Thirty-Seventh Posture: Right Kick with Heel. Here, left and right are reversed.

Figure 172

The Forty-Third Posture:
Turn Body, Kick with Right Heel

Movement One: With the right heel off the ground and using the ball of the right foot as a pivot, the body turns swiftly to the right rear. At the same time, the left foot, following the turning of the body, swings from the left out to the front and to the right, dropping down next to the ankle of the right foot, with the toes touching the ground first. Following, the center of gravity gradually shifts to the left leg until the whole foot is planted solidly. Thereupon, the left leg squats down slightly and the right foot lifts up. At the same time the two palms, following the turning of the body, collect from the left and right to intersect in front of the chest, with the right palm on the outside. The palms both face in. The eyes follow the turning of the body, looking levelly out. The vision must include the two palms closing in an embrace. (Figures 173–174)

Figure 173

Figure 174

Movement Two is the same as movement two for the Thirty-Seventh Posture: Right Kick with Heel. (Figure 175)

Important Points

1. Review the Important Points for the Thirty-Seventh Posture, Right Kick with Heel.

2. When turning the body, you must make use of the power of the right foot revolving (as soon as the foot begins revolving, the heel then leaves the ground) and of the swinging motion of the left leg. Only then can the turn to the

Figure 175

rear be swift, round, and graceful. When doing the turn, the body must not bend forward or lean backward, or you will be unstable.

3. The closing and intersecting of the palms must start and finish in accord with the turning motion of the body.

The Forty-Fourth Posture:
Advance Step, Deflect, Parry, and Punch

Movement One: The left leg gradually squats down. The right foot lowers down as the waist turns slightly right. At the same time, the right palm, changing to a fist, coils in an arc from the right downward, passing in front of the abdomen. The heart of the palm turns to face down. The left palm, following with the squatting down of the left leg, sinks down slightly, then arcs forward and upward from the left (the arc is no higher than the ear). The palm faces right and down. The eyes briefly attend to the right fist coiling left, then gradually turn to look forward evenly. (Figure 176)

Figure 176

Movements Two, Three, and *Four* are the same as movements three, four, and five of the Twelfth Posture, Advance Step, Deflect, Parry, and Punch. (See Figures 46–49.)

Important Points: Review the Important Points for the Twelfth Posture, Advance Step, Deflect, Parry, and Punch.

The Forty-Fifth Posture: Like Sealing, As If Closing

The movements and Important Points are identical to those of the Thirteenth Posture: Like Sealing, As If Closing. (See Figures 50–53.)

The Forty-Sixth Posture: Cross Hands

The movements and Important Points are identical to those of the Fourteenth Posture, Cross Hands. (See Figures 54–56.)

The Forty-Seventh Posture: Embrace Tiger, Return to Mountain

The movements and Important Points are identical to those of the Fifteenth Posture, Embrace Tiger, Return to Mountain. (See Figures 57–67.)

The Forty-Eighth Posture: Oblique Single Whip

The movements and Important Points are the same as those for the Fourth Posture, Single Whip, only the direction of the ending posture is toward the southeast instead of due east. (See Figure 68, then continue with Figures 177–179.)

Figure 177   Figure 178   Figure 179

The Forty-Ninth Posture: Wild Horse Parts Mane

Part One: Right Part the Mane

Movement One: The toes of the left foot turn in, planting solidly. The body turns slightly right. The center of gravity gradually shifts completely to the left leg, and the left leg sits solidly. The right foot draws in close to the ankle of the left foot and lifts up toward the front. At the same time the left palm, with the left elbow bent, moves in an arc to a point in front of the left chest. The right hook hand changes to a palm and moves in an arc from the right, then down toward the left, arriving in front of the abdomen. As it moves, the arm **rotates** out, causing the palm to turn and face left and up, forming a sphere-holding shape with the left hand.

The two arms both assume arc shapes. The vision attends to the left palm. (Figure 180)

Figure 180

Movement Two: The right foot steps out to the right (west, slightly to the north). The body gradually turns right. First let the heel touch the ground. Following, the center of gravity gradually shifts to the right leg, until the whole foot is solidly planted. Bend the right leg, and push from the left heel, forming a right bow stance. At the same time, following the turning of the body, the right palm, using the thumb side, splits out (*lie chu*) in an arc to the right and upward, to a height equal with the shoulder. The left palm plucks (*cai*) to the left in an arc and down to a position beside the left *kua*. The vision attends to the right palm splitting out, slightly in advance of the arrival point to the right of the right palm. (Figure 181)

Figure 181

Part Two: Left Part the Mane

Movement One: The toes of the right foot turn out, planting solidly. The body turns slightly right. The center of gravity gradually shifts entirely to the right leg. The right leg sits solidly. The left foot lifts up and forward, passing by the ankle of the right foot. At the same time the right palm, following the turning of the body, with the right elbow bent, moves to a point in front of the right chest. As it moves, the arm **rotates** in, causing the palm to turn and face down. The left palm moves in an arc to the right, arriving in front of the abdomen. As it moves, the arm **rotates** out, causing the palm to turn and face to the right and up, forming a sphere-holding shape with the right palm. The two arms both assume arc shapes. The eyes follow the turning of the body, gazing levelly out. The vision should include the right palm. (Figures 182–183)

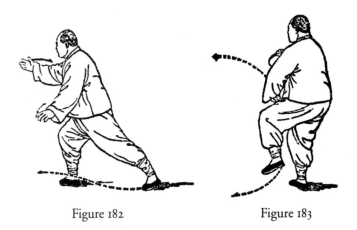

Figure 182   Figure 183

Movement Two: The left foot steps out to the left (west, slightly south). The body continues to turn left. Touch the ground first with the heel. Following, the center of gravity shifts to the left leg until the whole foot is planted solidly. Bend the left leg, and push from the right heel, forming a left bow stance. At the same time, following the turning of the body, the left palm splits out in an arc to the left and up, using the thumb side, to shoulder height. The right palm plucks to the right in an arc and down to a position beside the right *kua*. The vision attends to the left palm splitting out, slightly in advance of the arrival point to the left of the left palm. (Figure 184)

Part Three: Right Part the Mane

The movements are identical to those of Left Part the Mane, except left and right are reversed. (Figures 185–187)

Figure 184

Figure 185

Figure 186

Figure 187

Important Points

1. The bow stance of Wild Horse Parts Mane is a bit more open than the bow stances in general in the form, but it is not done on a 45-degree angle [i.e., to the corner]. The direction of the toe should be the same as that of the knee.

2. When the two palms are forming the sphere-holding shape, pay attention not to raise the elbows.

3. When either the right or left hand splits out, it must follow the turning movement of the waist. Also, the split movement must issue outward from the shoulder to the elbow, from the elbow to the hand, successively threaded together from joint to joint (*jie jie guan chuan*). Furthermore, the split movement, the turning of the body, and the transition to the bow stance must be coordinated and combined as one. The downward-plucking (*cai*) hand should not be too close to the thigh. The two arms must assume arc shapes.

The Fiftieth Posture: Grasp Sparrow's Tail

Part One: Left and Right Ward Off (*Peng*)

Movement One: The body turns slightly to the right. The center of gravity gradually shifts entirely to the right leg. The left foot lifts up to the right, passing by the inside ankle of the right foot. At the same time the right palm, following the turning of the body and with the right elbow bent and sinking, draws inward to a point in front of the right chest. As it draws in, the arm **rotates** in, causing the palm to gradually turn and face down. The right elbow sinks slightly, somewhat lower than the wrist. The left palm concurrently moves in an arc to a point in front of the abdomen. As it moves, the arm **rotates** out, causing the palm to turn and face rightward and upward. The two palms are opposite one another in a sphere-holding shape, the arms in curved arcs. The eyes follow the turning of the body and look out evenly. The vision should include the right arm. (Figure 188)

Movements Two, Three, and *Four* are identical with those of the Ward Off (*peng*) sequence in the Third Posture, Grasp Sparrow's Tail. (See Figures 6–9.)

Important Points are the same.

Part Two: Roll Back / Part Three: Press / and Part Four: Push

The movements and Important Points are the same as those explained in the Third Posture sequence: Grasp Sparrow's Tail. (See Figures 10–17.)

Figure 188

The Fifty-First Posture: Single Whip

The movements and Important Points are the same as those for the Fourth Posture, Single Whip. (See Figures 18–21, then continue with Figure 189.)

The Fifty-Second Posture: Jade Maiden Threads Shuttle

Figure 189

Part One: Left Thread the Shuttle

Movement One: The toes of the left foot turn in and plant solidly. At the same time, the right hook hand changes to a palm and arcs from the right toward the front and down. The left palm also gradually moves downward. (Figure 190)

Movement Two: The center of gravity shifts completely to the left leg. The body gradually turns right. The right foot lifts up. At the same time the right palm, following the turning of the body, arcs from below and leftward, passing before the chest and toward the right, and wards off upwardly (*peng*). The left palm continues to arc forward and downward. The vision attends to the right palm warding off upwardly to the right. (Figure 191)

Figure 190   Figure 191

Movement Three: The body continues to turn right. The right foot steps out to the right (west, slightly north), with the heel touching the ground first. Following, the center of gravity gradually shifts entirely to the right leg until the whole foot is planted solidly. The left foot lifts up toward the front, passing by the ankle of the right foot. Following the turning of the body, the left palm passes in front of the abdomen and moves to the right in an arc, arriving under the right forearm. The right palm, also following the turning of the body, continues warding off to the right. Then, sink the right elbow, naturally leading the movement of the right palm downward and back. The eyes briefly observe the right palm shifting back, then turn to look forward evenly. (Figures 192–193)

Movement Four: The left foot takes an oblique step out to the left front (southwest), with the heel touching the ground first. At the same time, the left forearm passes under the right forearm and wards off upwardly toward the front. The right palm (sinking the elbow), crosses [or "threads," *chuan*] back over the left forearm. As it threads back, the arm **rotates** in, causing the palm to gradually turn to face forward

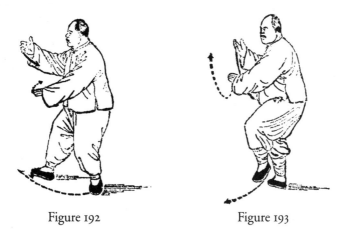

Figure 192   Figure 193

and downward. The eyes look evenly to the left front. The vision should include the left arm warding off to the front. (Figure 194)

Movement Five: The center of gravity gradually shifts toward the left leg. The left foot is planted solidly. The body gradually turns left. Bend the left leg, and push forward from the right heel, forming a left bow stance. At the same time, the left forearm moves upward, passing before the face. As it moves, the arm **rotates** in, causing the palm to turn and face forward and up. The left palm takes position in front of the forehead. The right palm concurrently pushes forward. The vision should include the right palm pushing forth. (Figure 195)

Figure 194   Figure 195

Part Two: Right Thread the Shuttle

Movement One: The toes of the left foot turn in, planting solidly. The body gradually turns right. At the same time the right palm, following the turning of the body, with the elbow bent and the arm horizontal (assuming an arc shape), moves before the chest. As it moves, the arm **rotates** out, causing the palm to gradually turn and face in. The left arm **rotates** out; the sinking of the left elbow naturally leads the movement of the left palm in shifting downward and also causes the palm to turn and face in. The vision attends to the left palm shifting back. (Figure 196)

Movement Two: The body continues to turn right; the center of gravity gradually shifts entirely to the left leg. The right foot lifts back, following with the turning movement of the body. At the same time the right arm, following the turning of the body, wards off to the right. The left palm, sinking the left elbow, passes over the right forearm then collects down and shifts back. The vision first connects with the left palm shifting down, then turns to look in front of the right arm. (Figure 197)

Movements Three and *Four* are the same as movements four and five of the preceding Left Thread the Shuttle, only left and right are reversed. The direction for the preceding Left Thread the Shuttle

Figure 196   Figure 197

is southwest, whereas the direction for this Right Thread the Shuttle is southeast. (Figures 198–199)

Figure 198   Figure 199

Part Three: Left Thread the Shuttle

Movement One: The center of gravity gradually shifts entirely to the right leg. The body turns slightly to the right. The left foot lifts up toward the front, passing by the side of the right foot's ankle. At the same time, following the turning of the body, the left palm with the arm bent at the elbow and horizontal (in an arc shape), moves in front of the chest. As it moves, the arm **rotates** out, causing the palm to gradually turn to face in. The right arm **rotates** out; the sinking of the elbow naturally guides the movement of the right palm in shifting downward, and causes the palm to gradually turn to face in. The eyes briefly watch the right palm shifting down, then turn to look in front of the left arm. (Figure 200)

Movements Two and *Three* are identical with movements four and five of the previous Left Thread the Shuttle, only the direction in

Figure 200

the previous sequence is southwest, whereas the direction of this Left Thread the Shuttle is northeast. (Figures 201–202)

Figure 201   Figure 202

Part Four: Right Thread the Shuttle

The movements are the same as for the previous Right Thread the Shuttle, only the direction of the previous one is southeast, whereas the direction of this Right Thread the Shuttle is northwest. (Figures 203–206)

Figure 203   Figure 204

Figure 205   Figure 206

Important Points

1. In all, there are four parts to Jade Maiden Threads Shuttle; their directions are to the four corners. Figures 195, 199, 202, and 206 are traced based upon original photographs of Master Yang Chengfu. When the original photographs were taken, they were shot in profile in order to obtain a clear line of vision. When practicing, however, the student should perform the postures to the corners.

2. With each turn of the body and each step, you must not rise up. The body should maintain vertical alignment. The movements should be linked together, even, with upper and lower following one another, coordinated and unified.

3. When the palm turns forward and up [in front of the forehead], you must prevent the leading [or "pulling," *yin*] shoulder from rising up and the elbow from lifting. The arm of the pushing hand must not extend straight—it must be slightly bent.

4. When changing to the bow stance and as the palm pushes forward, the toes, the forward knee, the body, the face, and the pushing palm should all be unified in facing to the corner.

The Fifty-Third Posture: Grasp Sparrow's Tail

Part One: Ward Off

Movement One: The center of gravity gradually shifts entirely to the right leg. The left foot lifts up toward the right, passing by the ankle of the right foot. At the same time the right palm, with the right elbow bending and sinking down, collects back to a point in front of the right chest. As it collects in, the arm **rotates** slightly out, causing the palm to turn and face down. The right elbow elbow sinks, somewhat lower than the wrist. The left palm concurrently moves in an arc to the right and down to a point in front of the abdomen. As it moves, the arm **rotates** out, causing the palm to turn and face to the right and up. The two palms face one another as though holding a sphere. The two arms assume arc shapes. The vision attends to the right arm. (Figure 5) [The narrative and figure reference here only refer to the transitional movements from Jade Maiden Threads the Shuttle to Grasp Sparrow's Tail. The remaining Ward Off movements are represented in Figures 6–9.— *translator*]

    Important Points are the same as for the Ward Off section of the Third Posture, Grasp Sparrow's Tail.

Parts Two, Three, and Four: Roll Back, Press, and Push

The movements and Important Points are the same as those in the Third Posture, Grasp Sparrow's Tail. (Refer to Figures 10–17.)

The Fifty-Fourth Posture: Single Whip

The movements and Important Points are identical to those for the Fourth Posture, Single Whip. (See Figures 18–21, continuing with Figure 105.)

The Fifty-Fifth Posture: Cloud Hands

The movements and Important Points are the same as for the Twenty-Eighth Posture, Cloud Hands. (See Figures 106–111, with the repetitions leading to Figure 112.)

Figure 207

The Fifty-Sixth Posture: Single Whip

The movements and Important Points are the same as those for the Twenty-Ninth Posture, Single Whip [as it follows the previous set of Cloud Hands]. (Figures 113–114, continuing with Figure 207)

The Fifty-Seventh Posture: Squatting Single Whip

Movements: The toes of the right foot turn out, planting solidly. The center of gravity gradually shifts toward the right leg. The right leg bends at the knee, squatting down, forming a left [empty] sinking stance (*pubu*). At the same time, the left palm follows the rearward shifting of the weight; with the elbow bending, it draws inward in an arc, passing before the chest, then downward, threading toward the front, following along the inside of the left leg. The vision attends to the left palm. (Figures 208–209)

Important Points

1. When the left palm collects inward and downward in an arc, it must be done in accord with the rearward shifting of the center of gravity, the relaxing of the waist and *kua*, the loosening of the shoulders, and the sinking of the elbow. Only in this manner will you be able to thread the movement joint by joint in leading the palm.

Figure 208   Figure 209

The drawing in and threading forward of the left palm must be rounded and lively. The fingers point forward (east), the palm faces south.

2. When performing the movements of Squatting Single Whip, you must prevent the body from leaning forward, from lowering the head, and from letting the buttocks stick out. You must maintain the vertical alignment of the upper body. You must also pay attention not to thrust out the chest.

3. When forming the left sinking stance, the left knee should be slightly bent—the left leg should not be forcibly straightened.

4. Although the vision follows the left palm, you should not lower the head when the palm proceeds downward and threads forward.

The Fifty-Eighth Posture: Golden Cock Stands on One Leg

Part One: Left Golden Cock

Movement One: The toes of the left foot turn out. The body gradually turns left. The center of gravity shifts forward and rises. The left leg flexes at the knee and bends forward, the right leg pushing straight. The right foot, with the heel first leaving the ground, comes forward with the lifting of the knee. Thereupon, the left leg gradually stands up, forming a left single-leg posture. At the same time, the left palm, following the forward lifting and leftward turning of the body, threads forward and upward, then brushes downward in an arc to beside the left *kua* (the palm facing down). The right hook hand, changing to a palm, moves downward from behind and follows the right leg forward as it lifts at the knee. Use the ulna side of the right forearm to press near to the upper side of the thigh of the right leg and lift (*tuo*) forward and upward in an arc. The arm bends at the elbow and arrives in front of the face, the fingers pointing up at shoulder height, the palm facing left. The eyes first attend to the left palm threading forward. At the time the left palm brushes left, they watch the right palm lifting upward. Then they look at the arrival point of the right palm, and evenly forward past the right palm. (Figures 210–212)

Figure 210

Figure 211

Figure 212

Part Two: Right Golden Cock

Movements: The left leg gradually bends at the knee and squats down. The body gradually turns right. The right foot lowers down beside the ankle of the left foot, with the toes touching the ground first and, following the gradual shifting of the center of gravity to the right foot, the whole right foot plants solidly. Thereupon, the heel of the left foot leaves the ground, and the knee lifts up and forward. The right leg accordingly stands up gradually, forming a right single-leg posture. While the left leg squats down and the right foot drops down, the right palm falls down in an arc to the side of the right *kua*, the palm facing down. The left palm moves forward from below; as the left leg lifts the knee forward, use the ulna side of the left forearm to press near to the upper side of the thigh of the left leg and lift upward in an arc, bending at the elbow and arriving in front of the face. The fingers point upward at shoulder height. The palm faces left. The eyes first observe the right palm lowering down, then shift to look at the left palm lifting up, briefly looking at the arrival point of the left palm, then past the palm to gaze evenly forward. (Figures 213–214)

Figure 213   Figure 214

Important Points

1. In rising from the left sinking stance of Squatting Single Whip, as the weight shifts forward, the left leg should gradually bend and the right leg should gradually push from the heel. Relax the waist and the *kua*. The upper body must shift forward simultaneously, then gradually lift forward while forming the shape of the left bow stance; it must not lift up from the two legs extending straight.

2. During the process of doing Left Golden Cock, you first need to stably bend the knee and sit solidly on the left leg. Then the right knee gradually lifts up toward the front. At the same time, you must not first straighten the left leg to standing and then raise the knee—this results in an uncoordinated appearance. Within the entire process of changing from Squatting Single Whip to Left Golden Cock Stands on One Leg, you must prevent the upper body from bending forward and must maintain vertical alignment.

3. When changing from Left Golden Cock to Right Golden Cock, pay attention that as you lower down the right foot, the left leg should squat down at the same time. It is not simply a case of the right foot lowering down and the left leg still remaining erect. When the left leg then lifts up the knee, the right leg must accordingly stand up gradually.

4. When performing the Golden Cock Stands on One Leg, you must "sink the shoulders and drop the elbows," "seat the wrists," "have a receptive and lively energy at the top of the head," and "sink the *qi* to the *dantian*." There must be "elbows and knees combined," that is, the elbow must form a vertical line with the knee and they must face the forward direction as one. When in the single-leg posture, the supporting leg should not exert strength in extending straight.

5. Within the explanatory narrative of Left and Right Golden Cock Stands on One Leg, the verb "lift" (*tuo*) is used in accordance with the martial applications of these postures. When training, however, you must not have the palm facing up as implied in the

meaning of the word *tuo*, but must have the fingers facing up. [Yang Chengfu's *Complete Book of the Essence and Applications of Taijiquan* sheds light on this. In describing the application, he states: "Quickly raise the left hand and lift (*tuo*) the opponent's elbow." The verb implies using the heel of the palm in the application.—*translator*]

The Fifty-Ninth Posture:
Left and Right Step Back Dispatch Monkey

Part One: Right Step Back Dispatch Monkey

Movement One: The right leg gradually bends the knee and squats down. The left foot lowers down, passing by the inside ankle of the right foot. At the same time, the right palm moves to the rear (slightly to the right) and shifts upward in an arc, arriving at shoulder height. The left palm shifts forward as the arm extends. As they move, the two arms **rotate** out, causing the two palms to turn and face up. The eyes watch the right palm shifting up to the right rear. (Figure 215)

Movement Two is the same as movement three in the Seventeenth Posture, Right Step Back Dispatch Monkey. (See Figures 77–78.)

Part Two: Left Step Back Dispatch Monkey, and Part Three: Right Step Back Dispatch Monkey

Figure 215

The movements are the same as for those in The Seventeen Posture. (See Figures 79–81, continuing with 76–77, then with Figure 82.)

Important Points are the same as for the previous Step Back Dispatch Monkey.

The Sixtieth Posture: Flying Obliquely

The movements and Important Points are the same as those for the Eighteenth Posture, Flying Obliquely. (See Figures 83–85.)

The Sixty-First Posture: Lift Hands Upward

The movements and Important Points are the same as for the Nineteenth Posture, Lift Hands Upward. (See Figures 86–87, continuing with Figures 25–27.)

The Sixty-Second Posture:
White Crane Displays Wings

The movements and Important Points are the same as for the Sixth Posture, White Crane Displays Wings. (See Figure 28.)

The Sixty-Third Posture:
Left Brush Knee Twist Step

The movements and Important Points are the same as for the Seventh Posture, Left Brush Knee Twist Step. (See Figures 29–33.)

The Sixty-Fourth Posture: Needle at Sea Bottom

The movements and Important Points are the same as for the Twenty-Second Posture, Needle at Sea Bottom. (See Figures 88–90.)

The Sixty-Fifth Posture: Fan Through Back

The movements and Important Points are the same as for the Twenty-Third Posture, Fan Through Back. (See Figures 91–92.)

The Sixty-Sixth Posture:
Turn Body, White Snake Darts Tongue

Movements One and *Two* are the same as those for movements one and two of the Twenty-Fourth Posture, Turn Body and Strike. (See Figures 93–94.)

Movement Three: The right foot drops down toward the front (slightly to the right), with the heel touching the ground first. Following, the center of gravity moves toward the right leg, gradually, until the entire foot plants solidly. Bend the right leg, push from the left heel—the left toes slightly turn in—forming a right bow stance as the body continues turning right. At the same time the right fist, changing to a palm, continues to follow the turning of the body and casts out and downward toward the front, arriving in front and to the right of the waist. The palm faces up. The left palm withdraws in an arc to a point in front of the chest and passes over the inner edge of the right forearm, pushing out toward the front. The eyes look forward evenly but must also make a connection with the left palm pushing forward. (Figures 216–217)

Figure 216

Figure 217

Important Points: Except for the right hand changing from a fist to a palm in movement three of this sequence, the remaining elements are all identical with Turn Body and Strike, so the Important Points are the same as for that sequence.

The Sixty-Seventh Posture: Deflect, Parry, and Punch

Movement One: The center of gravity gradually shifts toward the left leg; the body turns left. At the same time, the left elbow follows the turning of the body and sinks down. The left arm **rotates** out, causing the palm to gradually turn and face up. The right palm changes to a fist, extending forward and upward above the left palm. The vision attends to the right fist extending forward. (Continue with Figure 97.)

The remaining movements are identical with those of the Twenty-Fifth Posture, Advance Step, Deflect, Parry, and Punch. (Continue with Figures 98–103.)

Important Points are fundamentally the same as for Advance Step, Deflect, Parry, and Punch, only the linking movements involving the right palm's change to a fist are different. [I.e., in Advance Step, Deflect, Parry, and Punch, the right hand is already forming a fist.]

The Sixty-Eighth Posture: Grasp Sparrow's Tail

The movements and Important Points are the same as those for the Twenty-Sixth Posture, Step Up, Grasp Sparrow's Tail. (See Figure 104, continuing with Figures 8–17.)

The Sixty-Ninth Posture: Single Whip

The movements and Important Points are the same as those for the Twenty-Seventh Posture, Single Whip. (See Figures 18–21, continuing with Figure 105.)

The Seventieth Posture: Cloud Hands

The movements and Important Points are the same as those for the Twenty-Eighth Posture, Cloud Hands. (See Figures 106–112, and review the instructions for the three sections of Cloud Hands.)

The Seventy-First Posture: Single Whip

The movements and Important Points are the same as those for the Twenty-Ninth Posture, Single Whip. (See Figures 113–115.)

The Seventy-Second Posture: High Pat on Horse with Piercing Palm

Part One: High Pat on Horse

The movements and Important Points are the same as for the Thirtieth Posture, High Pat on Horse. (See Figures 116–117, continuing with [new] Figure 218.)

Figure 218

Part Two: Left Piercing Palm

Movements: The left foot lifts back. The right leg gradually squats downward. The left foot takes a step outward, with the heel touching the ground first. Following, the center of gravity gradually shifts toward the left leg until the whole left foot is planted solidly. Bend the left leg and push from the right heel, forming a left bow stance, while the body concurrently turns slightly right. At the same time that the left foot is lifting back, the right palm gradually bends at the elbow horizontally; the arm forms an arc shape, and the palm arcs to the left and down, withdrawing inward. As it withdraws, the arm **rotates** out, causing the palm to turn and face up. Just as the left arm pierces over the right palm, the right palm then turns again to face down with the rotating of the right arm. The right palm lowers to a point below the left armpit. The left palm, still facing up, pierces forth over the top of the right palm, at a height level with one's chin. The eyes briefly attend to the right palm withdrawing inward, then again gaze evenly forward. The gaze should also include the left palm piercing forward. (Figures 219–220)

Figure 219

Figure 220

Important Points

1. The movement of the left piercing palm should be coordinated with the forming of the left bow stance and with the rightward turning of the body.

2. When stepping forward, you must prevent the upper body from inclining forward. You must endeavor to "step like a cat moves," and must be lightly agile when lowering into the step.

3. When the left palm pierces forth, the right arm must assume an arc shape. You must reserve an empty space [or gap] under the right armpit; do not draw it up closed. If you draw it up closed and the arm is not arc-shaped, your posture will appear awkward, and you will not attain the requirement of roundness and fullness. In addition, in the midst of the movement transitions you may lose the meaning of roundness and liveliness.

The Seventy-Third Posture: Cross-Shaped Legs

Movement One: The toes of the left foot turn in, planting solidly; the body gradually turns right, and the center of gravity gradually shifts completely to the left leg. The right foot lifts back toward the left (the heel leaving the ground first). At the same time the left arm, bending at the elbow, shifts right, the palm turning in. The right palm passes on the outside of the left arm with the rightward turning of the body and closes in an embrace. As the palm closes in the embrace, the right arm **rotates** out, causing the palm to turn and face in. The two palms intersect in front of the chest. The eyes, following the turning of the body, gaze levelly to the right. The vision should include the closing embrace of the two palms. (Figures 221–222)

Figure 221   Figure 222

Movement Two is identical to movement two of the Thirty-Seventh Posture, Right Kick with Heel. (Figure 223)

Important Points are identical to those for Right Kick with Heel.

Note: The original method of practicing the sequence called Cross-Shaped Legs was as a single sweep lotus. The above-elucidated practice method was a final revision to the fixed posture by

Yang Chengfu. Currently, those practicing according to this method are quite widespread. Accordingly, this book incorporates the final revised version of the posture. However, in order to provide for the reader an understanding of the original training method, the following explanation is presented:

After Left Piercing Palm, the toes of the left foot turn in, planting solidly. The body gradually turns right. The center of gravity gradually shifts completely to the left leg. At the same time the left palm, with the arm bending at the elbow, follows the turning of the body and shifts right, passing before the face. The right palm remains under the left armpit. The body continues to turn right. The right foot sweeps out in an arc from the left to the right and forward, the knee slightly bent in a natural manner. The foot sweeps no higher than the shoulder. The back of the foot faces slightly toward the right. At the same time, the left palm moves from above to the right

then left, meeting the face of the right foot with a slap. The narrative below continues with Advance Step Punch Toward Groin. With regard to the linking movements, in the explanation for movement one, the only difference would have to do with taking the right palm from beneath the left armpit, passing it in front of the abdomen, and coiling to the left as it changes to a fist.

Figure 223

The Seventy-Fourth Posture:
Advance Step Punch Toward Groin

Movement One: The left leg gradually squats downward; the right foot lowers down. The body gradually turns right. At the same time, the right palm changes to a fist, coiling from the right, then down, passing in front of the abdomen. As it coils, the arm **rotates** in, causing the heart of the fist to turn and face down. The left palm, also following the squatting down of the left leg and the rightward turning of the body, sinks down and moves forward. The eyes briefly attend to the right fist, then gaze levelly forward. (Figure 224)

Movement Two: The toes of the right foot turn out (*pie*) to the right front (northwest) and step out obliquely, with the heel touching the ground first. Following, the center of gravity shifts toward the right leg until the whole foot is planted solidly. The body continues to turn right. Following the turning of the body, the right fist casts out from the left upward before the chest and to the right front. As it casts forth, the arm **rotates** out, causing the heart of the fist to turn and face up. The left palm concurrently follows the turning of the body and parries in an arc toward the right front, the palm facing right. The vision attends to the left palm's forward parry. (Figure 225)

Figure 224   Figure 225

Movement Three: The center of gravity gradually moves completely to the right leg. The left foot steps forward, passing by the inner ankle of the right foot, first touching the ground with the heel. The body continues to turn toward the right. At the same time the right fist, following the turning of the body, coils in an arc to the right rear, drawing to the side of the waist. The left palm brushes down from the front to the right. The eyes look evenly forward. The vision should include the left palm. (Figure 226)

Movement Four: The center of gravity gradually shifts toward the left leg, with the whole left foot gradually planting solidly. Bend the left leg, push from the right heel, forming a left bow stance. The body gradually turns left, slightly folding at the waist. At the same time, the left palm brushes leftward in an arc past the front of the left knee, arriving at the side of the knee. The right fist strikes forward at the height of the navel. The eyes gaze evenly forward. The vision should include the left palm brushing left and the right fist striking forward. (Figure 227)

Figure 226   Figure 227

Important Points are the same as for the Thirty-Fourth Posture, Advance Step, Plant Punch.

The Seventy-Fifth Posture:
Advance Step Grasp Sparrow's Tail

Part One: Ward Off (*Peng*)

Movement One: The toes of the left foot turn out, planting solidly. The center of gravity gradually shifts entirely to the left leg. The right leg lifts up toward the front. The body turns left as it straightens up [the waist "unfolds"]. At the same time the left palm, with the arm bending at the elbow, moves up in an arc from the left to a point in front of the left chest, the palm facing to the right and down. The right fist changes to a palm and folds in an arc from the front, arriving under the left palm. As it moves, the arm **rotates** out, causing the palm to turn and face leftward and up, forming a sphere-holding shape together with the left palm. Both arms form bow shapes. The eyes briefly look at the left forearm, then the right arm, then gaze evenly ahead. (Figure 7)

Movement Two is identical with movement four in the Grasp Sparrow's Tail sequence. (See Figures 8–9.)

Important Points are the same as those for Ward Off in the Grasp Sparrow's Tail sequence.

Part Two: Roll Back / Part Three: Press / and Part Four: Push

The movements and Important Points are all identical with those of the initial Grasp Sparrow's Tail sequence. (See Figures 10–17.)

The Seventy-Sixth Posture: Single Whip

The movements and Important Points are the same as those for the Fourth Posture, Single Whip. (See Figures 18–21, continuing with Figure 207.)

The Seventy-Seventh Posture: Squatting Single Whip

The movements and Important Points are the same as those for the Fifty-Seventh Posture, Squatting Single Whip. (See Figure 208, continuing with Figure 228.)

Figure 228

The Seventy-Eighth Posture: Step Up Seven Stars

Movements: The toes of the left foot turn out. The center of gravity gradually shifts forward to the left leg. The body gradually rises forward, turning left. The left leg bends at the knee, the right leg pushes from the heel. With the heel leaving the ground first, the right foot lifts up and forward, passing the inside ankle of the left foot, and takes a half-step out to the front. The toes touch the ground, forming a right empty stance. At the same time, the left palm sweeps up to a point in front of the chest, forming a fist. The right hook hand changes to a fist and, following the right foot, advances forward from the rear, passes the waist, and intersects with the underside of the left fist. Together, the two fists simultaneously ward off (*peng*) toward the front and upward. The two fists are at chin height. The heart of the left fist faces right, inclined inward; the heart of the right fist faces left and inclines inward. The eyes look evenly forward. The vision includes the intersection of the two fists warding off. (Figures 229–230)

Important Points

1. Review Important Point number one for the Fifty-Eighth Posture, Golden Cock Stands on One Leg.

2. In the process of forming the right empty stance from Squatting Single Whip, pay attention that the body does not sway to and

Figure 229   Figure 230

fro. You must preserve the vertical alignment of the upper torso, relaxing the waist and thighs. Guard against stiffening the waist as a strategy for maintaining balance. You must not use the toes of the right foot to aid in supporting the weight of the body, for in this instance the right foot is empty and the left foot is solid. If you exert any strength in touching the ground with the right toes, sharing in the support of the weight, this is committing the error of "double weighting," with no clear distinction between empty and solid.

3. As the right fist is warding off, it should be as if both warding off and striking. Pay attention not to produce merely a forward and upward waving gesture.

4. When the two fists are warding off upwardly, the shoulders must not rise or lock up as the fists intersect. The two arms must form arc shapes in order that the posture may achieve the requirements of *qu xu* (collecting and storing energy in curves) and *yuan man* (roundness and fullness).

The Seventy-Ninth Posture: Retreat Astride Tiger

Movements: The right foot retreats back a step, passing the inside ankle of the left foot. The body turns accordingly to the right. The center of gravity gradually shifts to the right foot. The left foot lifts slightly toward the rear, lowering down perhaps half a foot from its original position. Use the toes of the foot to touch the ground, forming a left empty stance. The body, accordingly, again turns toward the front. At the same time the two fists, changing to palms, separate and open to the left and right. The right palm, following the rightward turning of the body, arcs from the front downward, to the right, then upward, (this just as the body turns to face squarely forward), arriving to the right and above the body. As it arcs, the arm **rotates** in, causing the palm to turn toward the front (and slightly up). The left palm descends in an arc from in front, downward and to the left to arrive beside the left thigh. The palm faces down; the fingers point forward. The eyes first observe the right palm arcing to the right. Just as the right palm is moving upward, the eyes shift to gaze forward evenly. The vision should include the two palms. (Figures 231–232)

Figure 231

Figure 232

Important Points

1. When taking the retreating step back, pay attention to the landing point of the right foot; you must not plant it on a straight line [i.e., in line with the front foot].

2. While forming the posture Retreat Astride Tiger (Figure 232), the upper torso must not incline to the right or lean backward; one must remain in vertical alignment.

3. After the two palms separate and open, the arms must assume arc shapes. Pay attention that the two palms do not open out from the body too much or assume a loose appearance.

The Eightieth Posture: Turn Body Sweep Lotus

Movement One: The left palm moves in an arc from beside the left thigh to the left and up, arriving in front of the left forehead. The right palm moves in an arc from above to the right, then down, passing before the abdomen and arriving in front of the left chest. The palm faces downward and slightly to the front. (Figure 233)

Movement Two: Using the ball of the right foot as a pivot, the body turns to the right rear. The left foot, following, treads the ground very slightly, then lifts. The left leg, following the turning of the body, sweeps to the right and back. The two palms, following the turning of the body, shift toward the right rear. As they shift, the right palm gradually moves up to the height of the nose; the left palm gradually moves down to the height of the chest. The two palms both face down. The eyes, following the rotation of the body, gaze levelly ahead. (Figures 234–235)

Movement Three: The left foot lowers to the ground on an angle to the left front; the toes are turning in (northeast). Following, the center of gravity shifts gradually to the left leg until the entire foot is planted solidly. The body continues to turn rightward. The left leg bends at the knee and sits solidly. The ball of the right foot still touches the ground, as though in a right empty stance. The two palms continue shifting levelly to the right with the turning of the torso. The right palm moves to the right front of the body; the left palm moves to the left side of the right wrist, slightly lower than the right palm. The eyes gaze evenly forward as the body turns. The vision should include the two palms moving to the right. (Figure 236)

Movement Four: The waist turns from left to right. The right foot sweeps out in an arc from the left to the upper right, the knee slightly bent in a natural manner, and the foot going no higher than the shoulders. The back of the foot faces slightly toward the right. At the same time, the two palms move from the right to the left, meeting the back of the right foot with a slap (first the left, then the right—the body at this point turns from right to left). The vision attends to the two palms slapping the back of the foot. (Figures 237–238)

Figure 233   Figure 234   Figure 235

Figure 236   Figure 237   Figure 238

Important Points

1. When using the ball of the right foot as a pivot in turning the body to the right rear, you must take advantage of the left foot slightly treading the ground; only then can the sweeping of the leg to the right rear and the turning of the body have a round and lively turning force. While turning, the body must not sway to and fro; the body must stand in central equilibrium. However, the waist must not stiffen to accomplish this but must remain loosened (*fang song*).

2. When the left foot lowers to the ground, you must gradually lower into a squat, producing a form like a right empty stance. After that, as the waist turns from the left to the right and the right foot sweeps to the upper right, the leg gradually stands up, but still does not extend straight.

3. The Right Leg Sweep Lotus is an instance of transverse energy (*heng jin*); you must use the turning of the waist to lead the movement of the right leg's outward sweep. Since the right leg's outward sweep is *heng jin*, you want to use the waist to lead the movement; therefore it is best that the right foot not rise above the shoulders. At the same time, the right leg must not extend straight but must be slightly bent. If the leg is stretched straight and the height of the foot goes beyond the shoulders, then one will necessarily be using a greater measure of power from the *kua* (inner thigh) and less power from the waist. Conversely, with the leg slightly bent and the height of the foot not exceeding the shoulders, one can then fully utilize the power from the waist and achieve the requirements of *heng jin*. Furthermore, the energy that issues through the back of the foot will be even greater.

The Eighty-First Posture:
Draw the Bow and Shoot the Tiger

Movement One: The left leg gradually lowers into a squat. The body continues to turn left. The right foot lowers down to its original position (still slanted to the southeast). First let the heel touch the ground, then the center of gravity gradually shifts toward the right leg until the entire foot is planted solidly. At the same time the two palms, following the turning of the body, sweep levelly toward the left. The right arm accordingly **rotates** out, causing the palm to turn and face up. The vision attends to the leftward movement of the two palms. (Figure 239)

Figure 239

Movement Two: The body gradually turns right. Bend the right leg, and push from the left heel, forming a right bow stance. The two palms, following the turning of the body, coil from the left, passing down before the abdomen and toward the right, turning into fists, and continuing in an arc to the right and coiling upward. As the right fist coils, the arm **rotates** in, causing the heart of the right fist to gradually turn and face out. It passes the side of the right ear (at this point the body is turning from right to left) and strikes obliquely to the left front, at the height of the forehead. The fist arrives just in front of the right temple, the arm assuming an arc shape. As the left fist coils, the arm **rotates** in, causing the heart of the fist to turn and face down. The fist then strikes forth obliquely to the left front (again, at the point that the body is turning from the right to the left), passing in front of the chest. The fist is at a height even with the chest. The eyes first attend to the two hands coiling up to the right. Just as the body is turning left and the two fists are about to strike toward the left front, the eyes gaze evenly toward the left front. The vision should include the two fists striking forth. (Figures 240–241)

Figure 240   Figure 241

Important Points

1. The two hands must follow the turning motion of the waist. The waist, after the two hands have slapped the back of the right foot, turns first to the left, then to the right. The two hands also accordingly coil rightward and upward. As the right fist coils to the side of the right ear and the left fist coils to a point in front of the chest, the torso then changes to turn leftward, and the two fists again follow the torso's leftward turning as they strike forth obliquely to the left front. The body's turning motion, the two fists striking forth, and the change to a right bow stance all must be coordinated as one.

2. When executing Draw the Bow and Shoot the Tiger (Figure 241), you must prevent the right elbow from rising up, the shoulders from rising up, and the body from leaning forward.

The Eighty-Second Posture:
Advance Step, Deflect, Parry, and Punch

Movement One: The center of gravity gradually shifts to the left leg. The body gradually turns left. At the same time, the left fist changes to a palm and, following the turning of the body, rolls back (*lu*) to the left rear. As it rolls back, the arm **rotates** out, causing the palm to turn and face up. The right fist arcs forward, descending to a point just in front of and above the left palm. As it descends, the arm **rotates** out, causing the heart of the fist to turn and face leftward and inward (the right fist is at the height of the shoulder). The right fist follows the left palm in forming left roll back (*lu*). (See Figures 147–148.)

Movement Two: The center of gravity gradually moves entirely to the left leg. The right foot lifts back. At the same time, the right fist coils from the right front down, passing in front of the abdomen and to the left, the heart of the fist turning to face down. The left palm makes an arc to the left and up (no higher than the ear). As it arcs, the arm **rotates** in, causing the palm to turn and face rightward and downward. The vision briefly attends to the two hands' coiling, then gradually turns to face forward evenly. (See Figure 149, then 45.)

Movements Three, Four, and *Five* are the same as those movements in the Twelfth Posture, Advance Step, Deflect, Parry, and Punch. (See Figures 46–49.)

Important Points are the same as for the Twelfth Posture, Advance Step, Deflect, Parry, and Punch.

The Eighty-Third Posture: Like Sealing, As If Closing

The movements and Important Points are the same as for the Thirteenth Posture, Like Sealing, As If Closing. (See Figures 50–53.)

The Eighty-Fourth Posture: Cross Hands

The movements and Important Points are the same as for the Fourteenth Posture, Cross Hands. (See Figures 54–56.)

The Eighty-Fifth Posture: Closing Posture

Movements: The two palms extend forward, separating and opening, with the two hands shoulder-width apart. At the same time, the two arms **rotate** in, causing the two palms to turn and face down. Thereupon, the two elbows sink downward, naturally guiding the movement of the palms downward with slow, steady dignity. The palms push down to a position in front of the *kua*, the fingers facing forward, the palms still facing down. The eyes gaze levelly forward. (Figures 242–244)

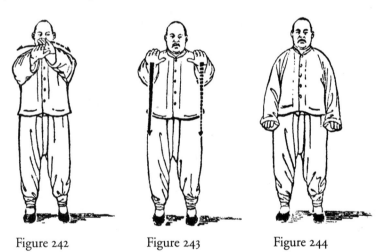

Figure 242   Figure 243   Figure 244

Important Points

1. The Important Points are the same as those for the Beginning Form.

2. Finally, the two arms, hands, and the fingers should hang down naturally.

162

Chapter Three

Yang Style Taijiquan
Push Hands

In Yang style Taijiquan there are three traditional push-hands methodologies. Herein a brief introduction is provided as a supplement.

Fixed-Step Push Hands (*Ding Bu Tuishou*)

Fixed-step Push Hands is also called Four-square Push Hands (*Si Zheng Tuishou*) and consists of two partners together using the four hand methods of *peng, lu, ji,* and *an,* proceeding in the original standing position. The movements are as follows:

1. Two partners, *A* and *B*, stand opposite one another. Each steps forward with the right foot. (For the convenience of explanation here, we are assuming that both step out with the right foot. During training, one can alternate by turns with the right and left foot in front.) Each raises the left hand to attach with the other's. The backs of the hands face each other, the wrists intersecting. Each contains *pengjin* (ward-off energy). Then each raises the right hand to touch (*fu,* stroke, soothe) the partner's left elbow, forming dual attached hands, intersecting at the left wrists. *B* bends his right leg in a forward bow, *A* bends his left leg, sitting back. At the same time *B* turns, making his two hands push toward *A*. *A* uses his left arm to ward off (*peng*), bearing the pushing force of his partner. At the same time *A*, going along with the force (*shun shi*), begins to turn his upper body leftward. (*Tuishou* Figure 1. *A* is dressed in black, *B* in white; *A* is warding off, *B* is applying *an* [push].)

2. *A* follows the pushing force of his partner, turning the upper body to the left while sitting back, his left wrist still warding off (*peng*) the pushing energy (*anjin*) of his partner; using the right

wrist to stick (*nian*) to his partner's left elbow, **A** rolls back (*lu*) to the left. While rolling back, the right arm **rotates** out. **B** then lets his right hand leave his partner's left elbow, shifting it to the inside of his own left elbow. (*Tuishou* Figure 2. **A** is doing roll back.)

Figure 1   Figure 2

3. **B**, going along (*shun*) with the roll-back force of his partner, uses the right palm to adhere to the inner side of his own left elbow, pressing (*ji*) toward **A**'s chest, at the same time bending the right leg sufficiently. **A** follows **B**'s pressing force, turning the waist to the right, and **rotating** the two arms in. (*Tuishou* Figure 3. **B** is applying *ji*.)

Figure 3   Figure 4

4. *A* follows the pressing force (*ji shi*) of his partner, his waist continuing to turn right. His body turns until it is square with the direction of *B*. At the same time, the two arms continue **rotating** in, then, using the right hand to connect to *B's* right hand, his left hand sinks down, dropping to the opponent's forearm near the elbow. The two hands concurrently push forward, while bending the right leg in a forward bow. *B* then uses his right arm to ward off (*peng*), bearing the pushing power of his partner. (*Tuishou* Figure 4. *A* pushes, *B* wards off.)

Subsequently, *B's* upper body turns right. Using his left hand to stick to *A's* right elbow, he wards off to the right. *A* again uses his left hand to adhere to the inside of his own right elbow, pressing forward. *B* then changes to the push (*an*) posture. *A* again replies, using his left arm to ward off the push. This process continues in a cycle of reciprocal pushing. If the upper arms circle in the opposite direction, the movements are as described in the preceding, only left and right are reversed.

Fixed-step push hands requires that when one partner is pressing (*ji*), he does it precisely as the bow stance is completed. When rolling back (*lu*), it is done precisely at the arrival point of sitting back. (If one presses when sitting back, or rolls back in a forward bow stance, these are both errors.) Ward off (*peng*) and push (*an*) are performed midway between the forward bow stance and sitting back.

Active-Step Push Hands (*Huo Bu Tuishou*)

Active-step *tuishou* is two people using the four hand methods of *peng, lu, ji,* and *an* in coordination with the stepping methods of advancing forward and retreating back, progressing in a cyclical practice pattern.

1. **Combined-step (*he bu*) method.** Supposing *A* and *B* both begin with their left foot forward, also forming dual attached hands. (Active-step *Tuishou* Figure 1A, starting point) Suppose *A* retreats while *B* advances. *A* lifts his right foot slightly forward, then lowers

it back to its original position. *B* concurrently lifts his left foot slightly back, then lowers it forward to its original position. Continuing, *A* retreats with the left foot, *B* advances the right foot. *A* again retreats with the right foot, *B* advances the left foot. (Step Figure 1A. It appears as though *A* retreats three steps, and *B* advances three steps. In actuality, however, in the first step the leg is slightly lifted, then lowered to its original position.) Next, change so that *B* retreats as *A* advances. (Step Figure 1B, starting point, then to the last step position of *A* and *B* in Figure 1A.) When *A* has retreated three steps, he lifts the left foot back, then lowers it forward to the original position (changing to advancing steps). *B* advances three steps, then lifts his right foot forward, lowering it back again to its original position (changing to retreating steps). Continuing on, *A* advances as *B* retreats, each taking two steps (Step Figure 1B), afterwards changing again to *A* retreating and *B* advancing. In this fashion, one advances, one retreats, in a cyclical training pattern.

   2. Loop-step (*taobu*) method. The two partners *A* and *B* stand opposite one another a step apart. (Step Figure 2A, starting point) Suppose *A* retreats as *B* advances. *B*'s left foot steps forward and is inserted to the inside of *A*'s right foot. Concurrently, *A*'s left foot retreats rearward a step. Continuing, *B* steps forward with his right foot, lowering it to the outside of *A*'s left foot. At the same time, *A*'s right foot retreats back a step. Continuing, *B* again steps forward with the left foot, inserting it to the inside of *A*'s right foot. Concurrently, *A*'s left foot retreats back a step. (Step Figure 2A) Afterwards, change to *B* retreating and *A* advancing. (Step Figure 2B, starting point, then to the last step position of *A* and *B* in Figure 2A.) When *A* has retreated three steps, his right foot loops from the outside of *B*'s left foot to the inside (changing to an advancing step). *B* concurrently lifts his right foot slightly forward, then lowers it to its original position (changing to a retreating step). Continuing, *A* advances as *B* retreats, each with two steps. (Step Figure 2B) Afterwards, change again to *A* retreating and *B* advancing. In this way one advances, one retreats, in a cyclical training pattern.

Active-Step *Tuishou* Step Indication Chart

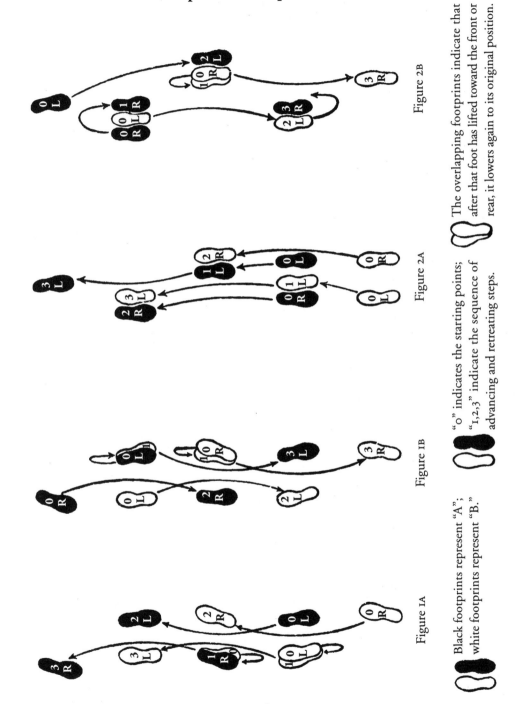

Figure 1A

Figure 1B

Figure 2A

Figure 2B

Black footprints represent "A"; white footprints represent "B."

"o" indicates the starting points; "1,2,3" indicate the sequence of advancing and retreating steps.

The overlapping footprints indicate that after that foot has lifted toward the front or rear, it lowers again to its original position.

In active-step *tuishou*, whether combined-step or loop-step, the upper arms still use the four hand methods of *peng, lu, ji,* and *an.* However, when initiating the movements, the retreating partner is inevitably performing *peng;* the advancing partner is performing *an.* Next, the retreating partner, as he retreats, performs *lu.* When *lu* reaches the point of completion, the steps are just retreating to the third step. The advancing partner, as he advances, changes to performing *ji. Ji* becomes complete just as the advancing steps reach completion. Next, as the retreating partner changes to advancing, the upper limbs also change from *lu* to doing *an.* As the advancing partner changes to retreating, his upper limbs also change from *ji* to doing *peng.* In this way, with the hand movements accompanying the step methods, one progresses in training.

Dalu

Because in *dalu* there are coordinated stepping methods, the range of the roll back (*lu*) is larger compared to *lu* in fixed-step *tuishou*, hence its name: Big Roll Back. Also, because the direction of steps in *dalu* is toward the four corners (see the complete directional tendencies in the schematic Figures 1–4), it is also named Four Corners *Tuishou* Method. Additionally, because its principal movements are *lu* and *kao* (shoulder stroke), and within each cycle the two partners in total have four *lu* and four *kao* movements, it is therefore also sometimes called Four *Lu* Four *Kao* (*si lu si kao*). The movements are as follows:

1. The two partners stand facing one another in north-south orientation. Suppose *A* is facing south and *B* facing north. The two partners form dual attached hands, the wrists of the right hands mutually intersecting. Now suppose that *A* is performing *lu*, *B* is performing *kao*, *A* retreating, *B* advancing. *B* changes to apply a dual-hand push (*an*) to *A*'s right forearm; *A* uses his right forearm to ward off (*peng*). (*Dalu* Figure 1. The movements in the explanation are done on the right side; those in the figures are done on the left.) *A* takes a retreating step with the right foot obliquely

Dalu Step-Method Directional Chart

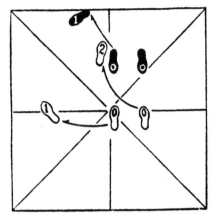

Figure 1A

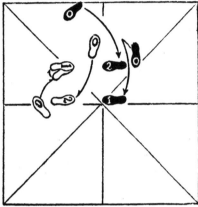

Figure 1B

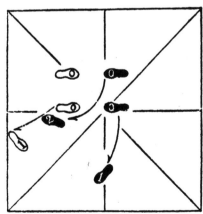

Figure 2A

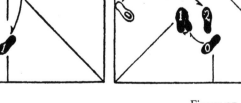

Figure 2B

Dalu Step-Method Directional Chart

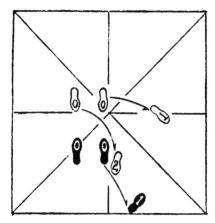

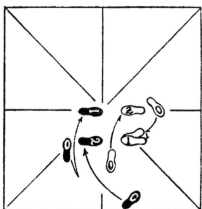

Figure 3A

Figure 3B

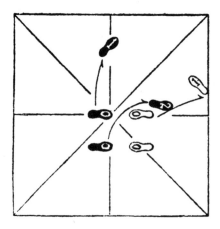

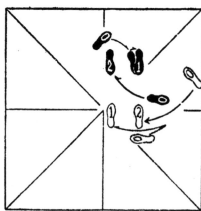

Figure 4A

Figure 4B

toward the northwest, his body turning right. At the same time, he turns out the right hand to pull down (*cai*) *B*'s right wrist (an empty grasp) and uses his left forearm (the ulna side, near the wrist) to stick to *B*'s right upper arm near the elbow joint, rolling back (*lu*) to the right. At the moment that *A* takes a retreating step, *B* takes a horizontal step toward the west (slightly north) with his left foot, following the force of *A*'s pull down (*cai*) and roll back (*lu*), and strides with the right foot, planting it below *A*'s crotch. At the same time, with the left palm shifting in close to the inside of the right elbow, he uses the sholder in the *kao* posture toward *A*'s chest. (For the step methods, see the *Dalu* Step Method Directional Tendencies Figure 1A; for the postures, see *Dalu* Figure 4. In the figures, Yang Chengfu is *B*. In all, there are five *dalu* posture reference figures, all drawn according to original photos of Yang Chengfu. Since there are no transitional movement figures, it is difficult to link them together. But the postures of left and right *lu* and *kao* are both represented, so they are included for reference. Among them, Figure 5 is from an even rarer photo, so it is included here.)

2. *A*'s left forearm follows the sinking of his waist, in order to transform and open *B*'s *kao* energy, and he uses his right hand to make a lightning strike (*shan*) toward *B*'s face. (*Dalu* Figure 3; Yang Chengfu is *A*. In this figure, *B* has not yet completed the *kao* movement; the step form should be the same as that of Yang Chengfu in *Dalu* Figure 4.)

3. *B* then uses his right wrist to connect with *A*'s right elbow, so that again he and *B* are forming the original dual-attached hands posture with the right wrists crossed. *B*, at the same time that he is connecting with *A*'s right wrist, uses the ball of his left foot as a pivot, turns his body to the right, retreats with the right foot, and again stands on the left foot, turning so he is facing east. *A* concurrently lifts his left foot slightly in, then turning the toes out to the north, sets the foot down. His body turns right and again steps right, turning so that he is facing west. (*Dalu* Step Method Figure 1B)

Dalu Figure 1

Dalu Figure 2

Dalu Figure 3

Dalu Figure 4

Dalu Figure 5

Each cycle of *dalu* should go through four corners. In the above narrative, **A** retreats, **B** advances; **A** rolls back, **B** does *kao*. Upon completing one corner, the partners complete one set of of *lu* and *kao* movements. Continuing the second *lu-kao* set, **B** retreats and **A** advances, **B** rolls back, **A** does *kao*. (The movements are as narrated above, only **A** and **B** change roles; the direction of **B's** retreating step is to the southwest. See *Dalu* Step Method Figure 2A.) **B** turns to face south, **A** faces north. (*Dalu* Step Method Figure 2B) The third time is also **A** retreating and **B** advancing; **A** rolling back and **B** doing *kao*, again turning to face east-west. (The movements are the same as the first time, only the direction is different. See *Dalu* Step Method Figures 3A and B.) The fourth part changes again to **B** retreating, **A** advancing; **B** rolling back, **A** doing *kao*; returning again to the original position of **A** facing south and **B** facing north. (The movements are the same as for the second part. See *Dalu* Step Method Figures 4A and B.) Practice proceeds like this in repeated cycles.

The above movement narrative begins with the intersection of the right wrists in the dual attached-hands form, so regardless of whether **A** or **B** is doing *lu* or *kao*, in both cases *lu* and *kao* are done to the right. If you want to do left *lu* and left *kao*, you can change to begin with the intersection of the left wrists in the dual attached-hands form, then proceed according to the above-explained movements with left and right reversed. (*Dalu* Figures 2 and 5) During practice, you may alternate left and right.

There are four principal hand methods in *dalu: cai* (pull down), *lie* (split), *zhou* (elbow-stroke), and *kao* (shoulder stroke). Within the context of training, the movements of *cai* (and simultaneously, *lu*) and *kao* are the most clearly evident. *Lie* and *zhou* by comparison, are not clearly evident. It is only within the transformations that they are applied.

***Lie* Method:** According to the explanation of *dalu* four-corner *tuishou* in Yang Chengfu's *Complete Book of the Essence and Applications of Taijiquan, lie* is introduced as follows: "... grasping the left wrist of **B** is *cai*. If the right hand does not move, then this is a 'compressing' (*qie jie*, lit., to 'cut off'). When transformed, it conveniently becomes *lie*. *Lie*, then, is to push away **B's** left elbow, and to use the palm to strike slantingly toward the base of **B's** neck." This explanation is assuming **A** rolling back to the left, and **B** performing left shoulder stroke. **A** uses his left hand to pull down (*cai*) **B's** left wrist. At the same time he uses the right forearm (ulna side, near the wrist) to stick to **B's** left upper arm (slightly above the elbow joint), rolling back to the left. If "the right hand does not move," then he uses the ulna to "compress" **B's** left elbow joint. If he "transforms in advantage to *lie*," then the right hand "pushes away **B's** left elbow," and with the thumb side of the back of the right hand, "strikes slantingly toward the base of **B's** neck." Because of this, the movements of *lie* are comparatively less evident. *Lie* is only present in the intent, or during the transformation. In this way, when using the back of the hand in a strike, this is "*lie*." Besides this, there are two additional ways of talking about *lie*. One way is to use the word *shan* (a "lightning strike") to describe the *lie* palm; another is, after **A** has rolled back, he follows through by sinking his right elbow, leading to the right to neutralize the *kao* energy of **B**. This is called *lie*.

Zhou Method: The movements of *zhou* are also within the intention or in the transformations. For instance, when **A** is rolling back to the left, using the right forearm to compress **B's** left elbow, **B** then folds his left elbow and sends it over the top of **A's** right forearm, butting **A's** chest with the point of the elbow; this is considered a movement of *zhou*. According to *The Complete Book of the Essence and Applications of Taijiquan*, "*Cai* power: **A** pulls down with the left hand but changes to *shan* [a lightning strike to the face]. The right arm continues to 'compress.' **B** folds the left elbow." From this sentence we can see that the subject of the roll back folds the elbow in order to apply the *zhou* method. However, there is yet another theory with regard to the rolling-back party using the *zhou* method, and it is simply that when **A** rolls back to the left, and at the time *B* performs left *kao*, *A* uses the right elbow to sink down and neutralize *B's* *kao* energy. This is considered a movement of *zhou*.

Although it is said that *dalu* is the four hand methods of *cai, lie, zhou,* and *kao,* in reality it also includes the hand techniques *peng, lu, ji,* and *an.* With regard to *peng, lie,* and *an,* they are discussed above. *Ji* (press) is just before the subject of roll back applies *kao*—the intention of *ji* is contained therein. In addition, during transformation, the person doing roll back can also apply *ji*; that is, after *A* rolls back to the left, he continues to use the right forearm to stick to *B's* left upper arm; he loosens the lower-pull down hand, shifting it to adhere to his right wrist. This becomes the *ji* posture.

Appendix

The Taijiquan Classics

Translator's Notes to the Taijiquan Classics

Taijiquan may be called an art in which one learns how to yield. In studying and translating the five short Taijiquan Classics appearing in this book, I discovered that I had to learn to *yield to the text*. By yielding to the text, I mean that I have endeavored to avoid imposing any preconceived notions of my own upon the text. My goal in translating these classics was to render as close to the bone as possible, without adding any verbiage that is not supported in the original, and without omitting anything that demands support in the translation.

There can be an advantage to a freer translation, in that a free rendering makes the text more accessible to the reader. I feel, though, that a freer translation also runs a greater risk of being interpretive. Moreover, these texts are difficult reading, meant to make the reader reflect on and ponder their meaning. One might say they are inter-active texts—the reader must engage with them in order to gain any benefit. My task, as I see it, is to get out of the way of the texts and to present them in such a way that they will stand on their own. If that means that some passages are vague and difficult to grasp, then it is up to the reader to navigate his or her way through them, as I have had to do with the originals. I have therefore avoided inserting implied sentence subjects when they are not clear in the originals, or replacing pronouns with nouns when the referents of the original pronouns are not explicit.

There are difficult passages, to be sure. I would suggest to the reader, however, to try to read these texts with a watchful eye for connected strands of ideas. Some of the received translations, and also some of the Chinese editions, break up the texts of the Taiji

Classics with interlinear annotations. While these can be helpful, they also have the effect of making the classics read like collections of aphorisms. In reading the originals, I discovered that they are in fact rather cohesive, with connections of meaning from phrase to phrase. The reader, of course, must find the thread, and strive not to lose it.

I have followed the arrangement and attributions of the texts as they appear in the Appendix of Fu Zhongwen's book. The issues surrounding the provenance of the Taiji Classics are beyond the scope of this project, but a few remarks are in order with regard to how they appear here.[1] As Douglas Wile has noted, the earliest published corpus of the classics associated with the Yang tradition shows "a considerable lack of textual stability. Although the language is quite consistent, it is variously distributed in different configurations and under different titles."[2] Indeed, the two texts appearing herein as "The Taijiquan Treatise" and "The Taijiquan Classic" (texts I and IV) appear with interchanged titles in some editions. To make matters worse, *both* of these documents appear in Fu's Appendix with the "Treatise" (*Lun*) title. In order to help the reader identify them as separate documents, I have titled the two texts in accordance with the titles they bear in most of the versions I've seen. I have followed Fu's placement of the section beginning with the words "What is Long Boxing?". In many versions, this appears as the last section of "The Taijiquan Classic," but Fu adds it to "The Taijiquan Treatise" instead.[3] Although I have retained Fu's placement, I have set this section off from the "Treatise" with a divided line because of the uncertainty of its rightful place, and because there is some reason to suspect it was originally a separate text in its own right.[4]

The Taiji Classics are beguiling and at times profound documents. Together, they appear to be made up of carefully written expository pieces and recorded bits of oral tradition. Parts of the oral tradition survive as rhymed verse that was probably chanted and memorized by the earliest masters, some of whom may have commanded marginal literacy. Some of the expository writings appear to have remnants of these mnemonic formulae within them, and these remnants sometimes present the greatest challenges for translation.

What Does "*Xu Ling Ding Jin*" Mean?

One of the most vexing phrases in this body of texts appears in Wang Zongyue's "The Taijiquan Treatise." This is the phrase that I've translated "An intangible and lively energy lifts the crown of the head." The actual phrase in Chinese is *xu ling ding jin*. *Xu* means "empty," "void," "abstract," "shapeless," or "insubstantial." *Ling* can mean "neck," "collar," "to lead," "to guide," or "to receive." *Ding* here means "the crown of the head." *Jin* is a word that should be familiar to most Taijiquan practitioners, meaning "energy" or "strength." To translate this phrase literally in a way that makes sense is seemingly impossible. To complicate matters, an alternate character for the second word in the phrase appears in some versions. This character is also pronounced *ling* but is pronounced with the second tone, while the other is pronounced with the third tone. This alternate character has the meanings "spirit," "wonderful," "mysterious," "clever," or "nimble." The version with this second *ling* character is notably the one that introduces the first of Yang Chengfu's "Ten Essentials of Taijiquan Theory." To demonstrate the difficulties presented in translating the phrase, I've assembled for comparison a number of different renderings:

Yang Jwing-Ming translates *xu ling ding jin* as:

"An insubstantial energy leads the head upward."[5]

T. T. Liang renders it:

"A light and nimble energy should be preserved on the top of the head."[6]

Benjamin Pang Jeng Lo translates the phrase:

"Effortlessly the *jin* reaches the headtop."[7]

Douglas Wile translates the phrase variously:

"The energy at the top of the head should be light and sensitive"[8] and,

"Open the energy at the crown of the head."9

Guttmann gives one rendering as,

"... the head is upheld with the intangible spirit."10

Elsewhere, he gives it a fairly plausible if incomprehensible literal rendering as a noun phrase:

"Empty dexterity's top energy."11

Huang Wen-Shan translates it as:

"The head-top should be emptied, alert, and straight."12

Robert Smith's version has it:

"The spirit of vitality reaches to the top of the head."13

Jou Tsung Hwa's rendering is similar:

"The spirit, or *shen*, reaches the top of the head."14

Finally, in one of the freer renderings I've seen, T. Y. Pang renders the phrase:

"The spine and head are held straight by strength, which is guided by the mind."15

As the reader can see, the range of nuance in these diverse translations of this one phrase is considerable. Virtually all of the readings are interpretive; that is, the four-character phrase as it has been handed down will not yield a dependable reading based upon the characters alone. One can only conclude that this phrase is a remnant of an oral formula whose original structure eludes our knowledge. Our understanding of it inevitably depends upon the context—the following phrase about sinking the *qi* to the *dantian*—and upon commentaries of former masters, including Yang Chengfu's elaboration in the first of his "Ten Essentials." The concept is also linked to differently worded but related phrases appearing in other classics, for example, "the spirit (*shen*) threads to the crown of the head" (*shen guan ding*) in the "Song of the Thirteen Postures," and the phrase about "suspending the crown of the head" (*ding tou xuan*) appearing in both "The Mental Elucidation of the Thirteen Postures" and "Song of the Thirteen Postures."

In my own struggle to understand the *xu ling ding jin* phrase, I looked at the possibility of reading the first two characters as a compound. In fact, there is a compound for *xu ling*, with the same *ling* character that appears in the Yang Chengfu version of the phrase. The Neo-Confucian philosopher Zhu Xi (1130–1200) used it as part of a phrase that means "an unclouded mind" (*xu ling bu mei*). Thomas Metzger's book *Escape from Predicament* can be a helpful guide in deciphering obscure Neo-Confucian formulae. He talks of the phrases *xu ling, zhi jue, xu ling zhi jue,* and *xu ling ming jue*, all of which he says interchangeably mean "intelligent awareness in its pure, naturally given, cosmically indivisible form, empty of any consciously specific concepts or sensations."[16] He also mentions the modern philosopher Tang Junyi's essay, "The Development of Ideas of Spiritual Value in Chinese Philosophy." Tang writes of *xu* and *ling*:

> "*Xu*" means to be vacuous and receptive. Confucius and Laozi spoke of *xu* mainly as a moral teaching. Zhuangzi, followed by Xunzi and the Neo-Confucianists, takes *xu* as one fundamental nature of the mind and connects it with the word *"ling,"* which means knowing freely, spontaneously, and without attachment. When the nature of the mind is seen as both vacuous and receptive, the sense of ego or of self as an individual differentiating itself from other things is uprooted in the depth of the mind.[17]

I subsequently read some commentary that points in a similar direction in Zeng Zhaoran's book, *Taijiquan quan shu* (Complete Book of Taijiquan).[18] Zeng talks specifically about this phrase, noting the variants of the *ling* character in the "common" editions of Taiji manuals, and saying that neither version of the commonly transmitted four-character phrase can really be explained. Zeng asserts that the *xu ling* phrase *is* an allusion to the Zhu Xi phrase meaning an unclouded mind (*xu ling bu mei*). In addition, Zeng cites variant characters for the second half of the phrase: *ding* (fix, determine) and *jing* (still, quiet), saying that they constitute an allusion to a phrase in the early Confucian text, *Da Xue* (The Great

Learning).[19] Zeng intimates that his version of the *xu ling ding jin* phrase is from a handwritten manuscript that he happened to read, and he implies that this reflected the original phrase.[20] Unfortunately, there is no way of confirming Zeng's findings, but they only serve to underscore the "textual instability" of which Wile speaks, and to highlight another stratum of possible nuances layered within the Taiji Classics.

My own rendering of the phrase depends upon context and available commentaries, including those from the important book by Meng Naichang, *Taijiquan pu yu mipu jiaozhu* (Taijiquan manuals and secret manuals with annotations). Meng writes that the phrase means "the ability to raise up the vital spirit" (*neng ti qi jingsheng*), that "it is intangible (*ruo you ruo wu*), and there must be no excess or deficiency."[21] Even the English word "intangible" is problematic, however, for it implies something that cannot be felt by the senses. What is being talked about here can definitely be felt, but the emphasis is on mind intent rather than on local, discrete muscles in the neck. The whole issue brings to mind Zhuangzi's wheelwright, who in talking about his craft said, "Not too gentle, not too hard—you can get in it your hand and feel it in your mind. You can't put it into words, and yet there's a knack to it somehow."[22]

The presence of Neo-Confucian language and concepts in the Taiji Classics, in the form of both verbatim and indirect allusions, is indisputable.[23] The language of the opening phrases and subsequent passages of Wang Zongyue's "Treatise" is clearly derived from Zhou Dunyi's (1017–1073) famous essay "Theory of the Taiji Diagram" (*taijitu shuo*).[24] Whoever assembled the more expository of the Taiji Classics was obviously literate and conversant with enduring cosmological and philosophical themes. Perhaps this is only indicative of the fact that such language was more or less the meat and potatoes of literate people in the late Ming and early Qing periods, but I am struck with how much the art of Taijiquan reflects the self-cultivation ethos of Neo-Confucianism and Daoism.

Other translation issues are somewhat less arcane than those addressed above. I will now discuss some of the issues of structure, words, and phrases as they appear in each of the five classics.

Taijiquan Lun

"The Taijiquan Treatise" is one of the more expository pieces. The document as a whole is not structured as verse, but it contains several pairs of four-, six-, and seven-character parallel phrases. Although clearly describing a martial art, the language is notable for being rather unmartial. For example, some translators have used the words "opponent" or "enemy" in the "Treatise" and elsewhere. The actual wording, however, is often rather more neutral; sometimes the noun *ren* (man, person, people) is used, or a pronoun, *bi*, meaning "the other." I have rendered both usages as "the other," as I think that this neutral language was deliberate in the original.

Another example of this neutral tone is found in the phrase that I've translated "This is to be a hero with no adversaries along the way." The key Chinese phrase here is *suo xiang wu di*, sometimes translated "invincible," or "undefeatable." The phrase's more literal meaning is "to encounter (or face) no significant opponent." To me, the more literal rendering reflects Laozi's words about the sage: "Because he does not contend, there is no one able to contend with him."[25] In like manner, the "Treatise" phrase reflects the ethos expressed in Sunzi's *The Art of Warfare:* "To win a hundred victories in a hundred battles is not the highest excellence; the highest excellence is to subdue the enemy's army without fighting at all."[26]

Still another example of neutral language in the "Treatise" is found in the sentence, "Observe a situation in which one who is aged can skillfully fend off (*yu*) a throng." The original meaning of the verb *yu* is "to drive a chariot." By extension, it carries the sense of "skillful." It has additional meanings of "to harness, to rein in"; "to resist, to keep out"; and "to control, to manage." Several translations render this "defeat," but I think that word is too strong and not strictly true to the text. Notably, there is not even a word for "opponents" or "attackers" in this phrase. The noun I have rendered as "throng" is *zhong,* whose meaning is simply "a crowd," "a multitude," or "masses."

The Taiji Classics use several different verbs for the crucial concepts of "following," "adhering," and "sticking." The verb I translate as "go with" (*shun*) can mean to go along with or to follow. Etymologically, *shun* means "water that follows a course"; "in the same direction as"; "with"; "obey" or "yield to."[27] The phrase in which it is used here, "I go along with the other," actually contains a character meaning "back" (*bei*), that is, the anatomical back. Some have rendered this verbally as "back up," connoting the action of the opponent. I find this problematic, however. It would be a most unusual usage for the *bei* character. This is another instance where the received wording probably reflects a remnant of an unrecoverable formula.[28]

We come now to the first instance of what I call the "threading" imagery in the Taiji Classics. In the "Treatise" it occurs in the sentence, "Although the transformations have innumerable strands, this principle makes them as one thread." The word I've translated here as "strand" is *duan,* meaning "an end" or "a detail, a particular." Etymologically, it means a tip or point, or a "sprout"—like an offshoot.[29] The word I've translated as "thread" is *guan,* and it appears more than once in the Taiji Classics, both nominally and verbally. The use of *"guan"* in the phrase here is closely similar to its usage in an important passage in the Confucian Analects which later Neo-Confucians put great store in. That passage is variously translated: "There is a oneness that strings my Way (*dao*) together." "My way (*dao*) is bound together with one continuous strand." "There is one thread that runs through my doctrines [*dao*]."[30] Confucius' disciple, Zengzi, responded to the statement, saying, "Yes." Edward Ch'ien, writing about the Neo-Confucian philosopher Zhu Xi's interpretation of this passage, states that:

> Confucius, according to Zhu Xi, saw that Zengzi had understood the individual principles in things and events, but was concerned that Zengzi might not have known that all these individual prin-

ciples formed a unity as the "oneness" of Principle.... Comparing the "oneness" of Confucius' Way to "a piece of thread" and the principles that Zengzi perceived in things and events to traditional Chinese coins which had a hole in the center, Zhu Xi said, "One must first accumulate a bunch of loose coins before one can proceed to string them together with a piece of thread."[31]

I strongly suspect that the line in "The Taijiquan Treatise" is an allusion to this Neo-Confucian meaning. In Arieh Breslow's *Beyond the Closed Door,* he recounts how "I once questioned Benjamin Pang Jeng Lo as to the meaning of the word 'one' in [the 'Treatise' passage].... It was a passage that had puzzled me for years. In reply to my query he said, 'Tao,' as though it were obvious."[32] Perhaps this background makes it even more obvious.

Another Neo-Confucian sentiment is expressed in the "Treatise" phrase about the need for "an exertion of effort over time" (*yong li zhi jiu*). "*Yong li,*" ironically, means literally to "use strength" and is the same compound as that in the famous Taiji aphorism, "Use mind, not strength (*yong yi, bu yong li*)." The meaning here, though, is to exert effort in self-examinination and study. Zhu Xi used the phrase in a moral sense. Metzger quotes the Neo-Confucian philosopher Wang Yangming, who said that to grasp the distinction between "heavenly principle and selfish desire," one "must constantly exert oneself (*yong li*) to examine oneself, overcome egotism, and master one's feelings; only then can one gradually gain some moral understanding."[33] It is significant that in an art that stresses non-exertion, we find a similarly strong exhortation to exert oneself in the cultivation of one's self.

An interesting usage is found in the sentence beginning, "Stand like a balance scale...." The characters for balance scale here are actually *ping* (level, even) *zhun* (measure, standard). The word *zhun* was used in early texts such as the *Zhuangzi* for a carpenter's level, which took as its "standard" the inherent ability of water to level itself.[34] I think, though, the image here is that of what is commonly called a steelyard, or scale suspended from above, which of course ties in with the imagery of the crown of the head being suspended. The actual Chinese term for a steelyard is *cheng* (which contains the *ping* element). However, when this was written, the term for steelyard may not yet have become standardized, or *ping zhun* may reflect a regional usage.

The same passage regarding the balance scale contains the famous admonition to avoid being "double weighted." There is a great deal of discussion among Taijiquan practitioners about exactly what this means, but the most helpful commentary that I've read is Meng Naichang's:

> There are two kinds of double weighting. There is double weighting between the other and myself and there is double weighting in my own body. Double weighting between the other and myself necessarily results in "butting" (*ding*). Double weighting in my own body necessarily results in stagnation (*zhi*).[35]

The notion of double weighting really rides on the preceding remarks about the action of the balance scale and the wheel, linking to the following sentences about the need to "know *yin* and *yang*." It is a keystone to the entire paragraph, in which we are told that "The foundation is to yield to the initiative of the other." This crucial concept, *she ji cong ren*, is a direct allusion to a passage in the *Mengzi* (Book of Mencius), in which it is used in a moral sense: "The great Shun had a still greater delight in what was good. He regarded virtue as the common property of himself and others, giving up his own way to follow that of others [*she ji cong ren*], and delighting to learn from others to practice what was good."[36] Here, then, we have a concept of moral action being appropriated into the ethos of a martial art and applied in the very mechanics of interactive movement.

Shi San Shi Ge

By far the most challenging of the five classics to translate is the "Song of the Thirteen Postures" (*Shi san shi ge*). Writings known as *ge* were not songs per se, but were rhymed verse formulae that could be chanted for easy memorization. This particular piece consists of twelve pairs of seven-character phrases. The last two pairs containing the remarks about the "one hundred forty words" refer to the preceding ten pairs. The verse form sometimes forces some very odd word order and character use, and one gets the sense that some of it is purposefully ambiguous.

The first phrase to consider is "The source of meaning is in the region of the waist." The words for "meaning" here are *ming yi*. As to the *meaning* of meaning here, this is really up to the reader to ponder. The words for "source" here are *yuan tou,* "the head, or source, of a stream." This imagery of the waist as the source of something that flows forth provides a very evocative image for the Taijiquan practitioner.

In the third stanza appears the phrase, "According with one's opponent, the transformations appear wondrous." Here, the word I've translated "opponent" is *di* in the original, which does indeed mean a rival or enemy. What I have translated as "according with" is the character *yin,* which can mean "cause, reason"; "for, because of"; "to follow"; and "in accordance with, on the basis of." The usage here is very similar to the concept of "according with the enemy" that Roger Ames elucidates in his introduction to *Sun-tzu: The Art of Warfare*. Ames writes, "The basic meaning of *yin* is responsiveness to one's context: to adapt oneself to a situation in such a manner as to take full advantage of the defining circumstances, and to avail oneself of the possibilities." Ames continues,

> *Yin* requires sensitivity and adaptability. Sensitivity is necessary to register the full range of forces that define one's situation, and, on the basis of this awareness, to anticipate the various possibilities that can ensue. Adaptability refers to the conscious fluidity of one's own disposition. One can only turn prevailing circumstances to account if one maintains an attitude of readiness and flexibility. One must adapt oneself to the enemy's changing posture as naturally and effortlessly as flowing water winding down a hillside.[37]

Clearly, the attributes of sensitivity and adaptability to circumstance are core concepts in the art of Taijiquan, but one can see that these concepts are rooted in the tradition that informed the *Sunzi*.

The line I have translated as "You will not get it without consciously expending a great deal of time and effort" can be rendered alternatively as "You *will* get it without wasting a great deal of time and effort." Both renderings can be defended as reasonable translations, and both make sense. The ambiguity is created by the word *fei*, which can mean "to expend" in a positive sense, or "to waste" in the negative sense. The key to understanding the phrase lies in the first half of the stanza about concentrating the mind. If this is done properly, one's time will not have been wasted, but in any event, one will have to expend time and effort.

More of the "threading" imagery discussed above occurs in the "Song of the Thirteen Postures" in the phrase "the spirit threads to the crown of the head." The verb is again *guan*, which can mean "to thread," "to link together," or "to pierce through." The phrase here refers to the effect resulting from the proper alignment described in the rest of the stanza.

There is a possible alternative reading for the phrase that I have rendered "to ceaselessly exert oneself in the method is self-cultivation." T. T. Liang, for example, translates this, "If one practices constantly and studies carefully, one's skill will take care of itself."[38] The last two characters in the phrase, *zi xiu*, could mean something like "it develops on its own," but more commonly *zi xiu* means "self-cultivation," which was a prevailing objective in Daoist and Neo-Confucian regimens. I am persuaded by the prevalence of other Daoist and Neo-Confucian themes in the Taiji Classics that this sentence is in fact an assertion that Taijiquan is an avenue for self-cultivation.

Shi San Shi Xing Gong Xin Jie

The text titled "The Mental Elucidation of the Thirteen Postures" combines body mechanical theory with recognizable self-cultivation themes. In fact, much of the language of the text is strongly reminiscent of a famous section of the *Mengzi* that was often referred to by Neo-Confucians as indication of an early concern for self-cultivation in the Confucian tradition. In that passage, Mengzi speaks of what he calls his "flood-like *qi*" (*hao ran zhi qi*). He makes it clear that moral energy is closely associated with the body's *qi*, and that it must be nurtured.[39] Mengzi elaborates, "The will is commander over the *qi* while the *qi* is that which fills the body."[40] The wording is different—"will" (*zhi*) carries more the sense of moral resolve than "mind/heart" (*xin*). The meaning, though, is quite similar to the opening line of "The Mental Elucidation": "Use the mind/heart (*xin*) to move the *qi*," and to the later lines, "The mind/heart (*xin*) is the commander, the *qi* is the signal flag, the waist is the directional banner," and "First in the mind/heart (*xin*), then in the body." When asked what he was good at, Mengzi said, "I have insight into words. I am good at cultivating my 'flood-like *qi*'."[41] When asked what he meant, Mengzi replied, "It is difficult to explain. This is a *qi* which is, in the highest degree, vast and unyielding. Nourish it with integrity and place no obstacle in its path and it will fill the space between Heaven and Earth."[42] The "Mental Elucidation" line about *qi* that I've translated as "cultivated in a straightforward manner, there will be no harm" is a direct allusion to this last sentence, taking the phrase *yi zhi yang er wu hai* word-for-word from the *Mengzi* passage.[43] The Neo-Confucian philosopher Zhu Xi remarked on this passage, "The adjective 'enlightened' fails to describe the *hao ran zhi qi*. Once we speak of it, we get the idea of wideness, greatness, endurance and strength, like a great river in its vast on-coming flow."[44] This understanding is echoed in the phrase in the "Mental Elucidation" that one should "… move like a flowing river." Even the closing lines of the "Mental Elucidation" advising that "the intent (*yi*) is on the spirit of vitality (*jing shen*), not on the *qi*," appear to reflect Mengzi's admonition about *hao ran zhi qi*: "At the same time, while you must never let it out of your mind, you must not forcibly help it grow either. You must not be like the man from Song. There was a man from Song who pulled at his rice plants because he was worried about their failure to grow."[45] The rice plants, needless to say, died as a result of the man's over-anxious efforts to aid their growth.

The "Mental Elucidation," perhaps to a greater degree than the other Taiji Classics, evinces a profound understanding of the integration of mind and body. It contains countless movement insights and marvelous imagery. The line "One's form is like a hawk seizing a rabbit," for example, is reminiscent of a Chinese expression meaning "bold and agile," often used to describe fine calligraphy. That expression, *tu qi hu luo*, literally means "the rabbit rises as the hawk lowers down"; in other words, the two actions occur instantaneously, as one motion. The subtlety of martial skill is revealed in such phrases as "To gather in is in fact to release." This has sometimes been translated as something like, "To withdraw is also to attack," but the original words, *shou ji shi fang*, carry none of the harshness of "attack." The notion of attack is quite out of keeping with an art that yields to the initiative of the other. The intriguing statement that "If the other does not move, I do not move. If the other moves slightly, I move first" is another bit of Taiji wisdom having an antecedent in the *Sunzi*. The formula in that text is, "Set out after he does, yet arrive before him (*hou ren fa, xian ren zhi*)."[46]

Taijiquan Jing

The document titled "The Taijiquan Classic" (*Taijiquan Jing*) has traditionally been attributed to a semi-mythical figure named Zhang Sanfeng. Its attribution to Wu Yuxiang (1812?–1880?) in Fu's Appendix reflects the scholarship that was deemed the most reliable at the time Fu's book was published.[47] In this document, we find two more instances of "threading" imagery: in the opening statement that the body "must be threaded together" (*guan chuan*), and again near the end of the text: "The entire body is threaded together joint by joint (*jie jie guan chuan*)." The compound verb *guan chuan* was traditionally used to describe the threading together of Chinese coins through the square holes in the middle to facilitate large exchanges of cash. Some of the received translations of the "Classic" add the words "like a string of pearls." There is, however, no mention of pearls in the Classic, and the imagery is more properly that of the slinky, linked coins. If you imagine handling these heavy strings of cash, and their behavior in the force of gravity, you can see that this imagery would be very effective for conveying the concept to early Taiji students. In Chen Weiming's commentary on this passage, he likened the effect of being threaded together joint by joint to the action of the Changshan snake discussed in Sunzi's *The Art of Warfare*. Therein we find, "If you strike its head, its tail comes to its aid; if you strike its tail, its head comes to its aid; if you strike its middle, both head and tail come to its aid."[48]

As for the sentence that I've translated, "The *qi* should be roused and made vibrant," the characters are *gu*, which at root means a drum and can mean to rouse or stir up, and *dang*, which is a very interesting character in itself. It means to move, to disturb, or to agitate, but in the sense of a sympathetic vibration. For example, it appears in the *Yi Jing* in a phrase describing the interactions of the eight trigrams (*ba gua xiang dang*). It also can mean "to cleanse," as etymologically it refers to a large tub. It is closely related to a character meaning "vast," or again, "agitated," like the ripples on water. The compound *gu dang* can mean "excited."[49] I have tried to capture the root meanings of the rousing effect of a drum and the resulting feeling of vibrancy, that is, pulsating with life, responsive and sensitive. This, I believe, is really the sense of the original.

Some translators have placed a noun or a noun phrase at the beginning of the sentence that begins, "It is rooted in the feet...," but the original of this particular document has only a pronoun and does not make explicit what "it" is. In his discussion about the movement of *jin* in the Grasp Sparrow's Tail sequence, Fu Zhongwen quotes this line from "The Taijiquan Treatise," making it quite clear that he thinks it refers to *jin*. Some of the other classic texts support the idea that when we talk about moving in Taijiquan, we are talking about moving *jin*.[50] Since this particular text does not mention *jin*, however, I will not introduce it into the translation. The reader must ponder for him- or herself what the text is saying and contemplate how to achieve "complete integration into one *qi*" (*wan zheng yi qi*).

The prescribed integration allows one to "seize the opportunity and the strategic advantage" (*de ji de shi*). Here again we encounter a phrase that suggests inspiration from the larger philosophical tradition. To *de ji* is to "obtain the opportunity." The character *ji* carries considerable semantic weight in early Daoist texts. Roger Ames speaks of its usage in the early Han compendium, the *Huainanzi*, saying that the range of meanings of *ji* extends to:

"critical point," "turning point," "pivot," "danger," and hence to "impetus," "motive force," "trigger," "clever device." Finally, *ji* means "opportunity," and, describing the person who is able to seize the opportunity, "adroit," "flexible," "ingenious."[51]

The sage as described in the *Huainanzi* is acutely attuned to this turning point and, says Ames, acts "as a collaborator with the natural processes by keeping his finger on the trigger (*ji*)."[52] The closing words of the *Huainanzi's* first chapter describe this ability:

Hence, the sage nurtures his spirit, harmonizes and retains the fluency of his *qi*, calms his body, and sinks and floats, rises and falls with *dao*.

Placidly, giving it its head,
When borne down upon, he makes use of it.
When he gives it its head, it is like shedding a coat;
In using it, it is like touching off a trigger [*fa ji*].

Thus, of the myriad transformations of things, there is none that he cannot match; of the hundred changes of affairs, there is none to which he cannot respond.[53]

The second half of our phrase, *de shi*, "to obtain the strategic advantage," is also embedded in an important antecedent tradition.

Ames identifies "strategic advantage" (*shi*) as "the key and defining idea in the *Sun-tzu: The Art of Warfare*...."[54] The concept threads throughout the *Sunzi* and is elaborated with a number of images, including this description of the expert at battle: "His strategic advantage (*shi*) is like a drawn crossbow and his timing is like releasing the trigger [*fa ji*]."[55] From this recurrent reference to "releasing the trigger" one can see how closely linked are the ideas of strategic advantage (*shi*) and opportunity (*ji*) in early Chinese texts. Thus it would appear that the conjoining of the concepts in "The Taijiquan Classic" phrase, *de ji de shi*, is not merely coincidental.

The notion of the pivot, the turning point, the critical point, is given additional treatment in the passage near the end of the Classic, "Each point has its point of insubstantial/substantial. Everywhere there is always this one insubstantial/substantial." At the risk of awkward and obscure phrasing in English, I have adhered very closely to the original wording, for I feel that this is a critical phrase in the text. As a classical commentator would say, it "rides" on the preceding phrase about the need to distinguish clearly. The operative word is *chu*, which means "a place; a spot; a point; a location; a locality." The original is a pair of seven-character phrases:

Yi chu you yi chu xu shi. Chu chu zong ci yi xu shi.

A word-for-word rendering would be:

One/point/have/one/point/empty/full. Point/point/always/this/one/empty/full.

The reduplication of the noun in the second phrase means "everywhere" or "in all respects" (a common convention in classical and modern Chinese). Note that there is no mention of "body" or "movement" in this phrase. One way of clearly distinguishing the substantial from the insubstantial is to find the still point in the movement, the fulcrum of the lever, etc. This is most essentially the waist, the proximal point, but it can additionally be the point of contact with the partner in one's arm, wrist, or elsewhere. This passage suggests to me that in distinguishing insubstantial and substantial, empty and full, *yin* and *yang*, one's concentration is at a finer level of concentration than "body" or "movement"; it is focused on this still point within the movement. The conjoining of the words "insubstantial" (*xu*) and "substantial" (*shi*), I think, helps to reflect the notion that "*Yang* does not leave *yin; yin* does not leave *yang*."

Da Shou Ge

The last text to consider is commonly known as "The Song of Pushing Hands."[56] This text is a grouping of six seven-character phrases. The wording is extremely economical. The phrase about upper and lower following one another refers to the integration of one's upper and lower body. Meng Naichang's commentary on this line is:

> 'Upper and lower follow one another' means one strand (*yi bu*) of completely integrated *jin*—a key point meaning the upper and lower limbs must not work independently, but are evenly coordinated as one with the movement of the waist.... If the hands, feet, waist, and legs do not act together, there will necessarily be a weak point, easily controlled by the other.[57]

Conversely, of course, if one avoids this weak point, one's partner or opponent has difficulty advancing and seizing the advantage.

"The Song of Pushing Hands" is probably the source of one of the most famous aphorisms in the Taijiquan tradition, *si liang bo qian jin*, "four ounces deflect a thousand pounds." The same phrase appears in "The Taijiquan Treatise," clearly as a quotation. In the Song, however, there are an additional two preceding characters, so that the phrase is: *qian dong si liang bo qian jin*. The first character, *qian*, means "to pull," "to haul," "to drag." It contains the ox radical, and commentators on this passage sometimes make reference to the action of leading a bull by the nose. There is in fact a compound, *qian niu:* "to lead an ox," which is also the name of a constellation, the Herdboy. The character following *qian* is a garden-variety verb, *dong*, "to move." I think, though, that in this passage it has a nominal function. Hence: "Lead [the other's] movement [using] four ounces [to] deflect one thousand pounds."

No less important a phrase is, "Attract him into emptiness, join, then issue" (*yin jin luo kong he ji chu*). Unfortunately, some translations have glossed over the subtle sequence of technique suggested in the original, leaving out the crucial "join" and reducing the concept to a formulaic "use withdraw-attack."[58] As noted above, "attack," which connotes an initiation of action against the other, seems antithetical to the Taiji ethos of yielding to the initiative of the other.

"The Song of Pushing Hands" is probably the oldest of the five classics assembled here, but it distills in its few words the essence of the art. Li Yiyu (1832–1892), in his "Essentials of the Practice of Form and Push Hands" (*Zou jia da shou xing gong yao yan*), takes the "attract into emptiness" and "four ounces deflect a thousand pounds" lines as the basis for an extended meditation on the fundamental features of Taijiquan. As he states, "The words are simple, but the meaning is complete."[59] In his remarkable essay, Li Yiyu brings together the most essential concepts from the core Taiji Classics, summarizing their significance by saying that "Practicing the form every day is the *gongfu* of knowing yourself," and that "Push hands is the *gongfu* of knowing others."[60] Significantly, the final line in his essay is a direct allusion to Sunzi's *The Art of Warfare*, "Know yourself and know others: in one hundred battles you will win one hundred times."[61]

I have been fortunate to be able to consult several translations of these classics. For the most part, however, I have done so *after* rendering directly from the original Chinese, or when I came up against a particularly sticky phrase. Even then, I would go back to the original and try to determine how another translator arrived at a given reading, and ask myself if that reading worked or not. Because of the nature of these texts, I do not believe that there can be a definitive English version of the Taiji Classics. For that reason, I encourage the reader to consider the renderings here and to compare them with other available translations. If, through this process, the practitioner gains a bit of new insight into Taijiquan principles or is led to previously unexplored avenues of investigation, then my efforts here will not have been in vain.

Notes

1. The best study in English to date on the issues and controversies surrounding the authorship of the core received classics is Douglas Wile's *Lost T'ai-chi Classics from the Late Ch'ing Dynasty* (Albany: State University of New York Press, 1996). See especially the sections treating the "Textual Tradition of the T'ai-chi Classics," pp. 33–38, and "Authorship of the Previously Received Classics," pp. 95–102.

2. *Ibid.,* p. 33.

3. See Wile, *Lost T'ai-chi Classics from the Late Ch'ing Dynasty*, p. 35.

4. Wile, *Lost T'ai-chi Classics from the Late Ch'ing Dynasty*, p. 33.

5. Yang Jwing-Ming, *Advanced Yang Style Tai Chi Chuan: Vol. One* (Jamaica Plain: YMAA, 1987), p. 218.

6. T. T. Liang, *T'ai Chi Ch'uan for Health and Self-Defense: Philosophy and Practice* (New York: Vintage, 1974), pp. 35, 62. Liang also refers to "The Light and Alert Energy on the Top of the Head" on p. 101.

7. Benjamin Pang Jeng Lo, et al., *The Essence of T'ai Chi Ch'uan: The Literary Tradition* (Berkeley: North Atlantic Books, 1979), p. 33. I've changed the transliteration from Wade-Giles to *pinyin* for the word *jin*.

8. Douglas Wile, *T'ai-chi Touchstones: Yang Family Secret Transmission* (Brooklyn: Sweet Ch'i Press, 1983), p. 11.

9. Wile, *Lost T'ai-chi Classics from the Late Ch'ing Dynasty*, pp. 44, 47, 163.

10. Guttmann, *The T'ai Chi Boxing Chronicle* (Berkeley: North Atlantic Books, 1994), p. 17.

11. *Ibid.,* p. 97.

12. Huang Wen-Shan, *Fundamentals of T'ai Chi Ch'uan* (Hong Kong: South Sky, 1974), p. 427.

13. Cheng Man-ch'ing and Robert W. Smith, *T'ai-Chi: The "Supreme Ultimate" Exercise for Health, Sport, and Self-Defense* (Rutland: Tuttle, 1967), p. 109. Smith seems here to have interjected the notion of "spirit of vitality" or *jing shen* into this phrase.

14. Jou Tsung Hwa, *The Tao of Tai-Chi Chuan: Way to Rejuvenation*

(Warwick: Tai Chi Foundation, 1988), p. 182. The character *shen* does not, in fact, appear in this phrase.

15. T. Y. Pang, *On Tai Chi Chuan* (Bellingham: Azalea Press, 1987), p. 145.

16. Thomas A. Metzger, *Escape from Predicament: Neo-Confucianism and China's Evolving Political Culture* (New York: Columbia University Press, 1977), p. 255, n. 64.

17. T'ang Chun-i, "The Development of Ideas of Spiritual Value in Chinese Philosophy," pp. 271–272 in Charles A. Moore, ed., *The Chinese Mind: Essentials of Chinese Philosophy and Culture* (Honolulu: The University Press of Hawaii, 1968). I have changed the romanization to *pinyin* in the quotation. Compare Allan, *The Way of Water and Sprouts of Virtue,* in which she explains that *xu* means "empty of sediment": "Water's ability to empty itself of sediment when still and thus become reflective is particularly important in Daoist conceptions of the mind/heart (*xin*) and the terms still, *jing,* empty, *xu,* clear, *ming,* are all important in Daoist descriptions of the mind/heart...," p. 53.

18. Zeng Zhaoran, *Taijiquan quan shu* (Taibei: Hua Lian Chubanshe, 1960), p. 30, and p. 55, note 1.

19. For commentary and partial translation of *The Great Learning,* see Wing-tsit Chan, *A Source Book in Chinese Philosophy* (Princeton: Princeton University Press, 1963), pp. 84–94.

20. Zeng Zhaoran, *Taijiquan quan shu,* p. 30.

21. Meng Naichang, *Taijiquan pu yu mipu jiaozhu* (Hong Kong: Haifeng Chubanshe, 1993), p. 6. This and subsequent translations from this book are mine.

22. Burton Watson, trans., *The Complete Works of Chuang Tzu* (New York: Columbia University Press, 1968), p. 153.

23. See, for example, the chart on pp. 158–159 in Wile's *Lost T'ai-chi Classics from the Late Ch'ing Dynasty,* in which he identifies many of the allusions to Neo-Confucian and other sources.

24. For a partial translation, see Wing-tsit Chan, *A Source Book in Chinese Philosophy,* pp. 463–465. For a sensitive treatment of how Zhou Dunyi's philosophical ideas bear on Taijiquan, see Arieh Lev Breslow, *Beyond the Closed Door: Chinese Culture and the Creation of T'ai Chi Ch'uan* (Jerusalem: Almond Blossom Press, 1995), pp. 148–157, et passim.

25. *Dao De Jing,* ch. 66, translation from Sarah Allan, *The Way of*

Water and Sprouts of Virtue (Albany: State University of New York Press, 1997), p. 138. See also her translation of *Dao De Jing*, ch. 68, p. 139: "One who is good as a knight is not belligerent. One who is good at battle is not roused to anger. One who is good at overcoming an enemy does not confront him. . . . This is what is meant by the virtue (or potency—*de*) of not contending (*bu zheng*), what is meant by the power (*li*) of making use of others."

26. Roger T. Ames, trans., *Sun-tzu: The Art of Warfare* (New York: Ballantine Books, 1993), p. 111. See also the following quote from ch. 12, p. 166: "A ruler cannot mobilize his armies in a rage; a commander cannot incite a battle in the heat of the moment. Move if it is to your advantage; bide your time if it is not. A person in a fit of rage can be restored to good humor and a person in the heat of passion can be restored to good cheer, but a state that has perished cannot be revived, and the dead cannot be brought back to life."

27. See Sarah Allan, *The Way of Water and Sprouts of Virtue*, pp. 92, 135.

28. See Wile, *Lost T'ai-chi Classics from the Late Ch'ing Dynasty*, in which he translates a document by Wu Ruqing having these characters, *shun* and *bei*. Wile translates the two as contrasting verbs: ". . . my opponent goes against the flow, whereas I go with it." I find this a highly plausible interpretation. Another interpretation is that of Meng Naichang, who says that *bei* means to "become passive" (*bei dong*), or lose the initiative, allowing the more skilled partner to "seize the center" of the opponent, and follow. *Op cit.*, p. 4.

29. For some interesting background on the philosophical usage of the character *duan*, see Sarah Allan, *The Way of Water and Sprouts of Virtue*, pp. 113–114.

30. These translations are, respectively, those of Edward T. Ch'ien, *Chiao Hung and the Restructuring of Neo-Confucianism in the Late Ming* (New York: Columbia University Press, 1986), p. 254; Roger T. Ames and Henry Rosemont, Jr., *The Analects of Confucius: A Philosophical Translation* (New York: Ballantine, 1998), p. 92; and Wing-tsit Chan *A Source Book in Chinese Philosophy*, p. 27.

31. Edward T. Ch'ien, *Chiao Hung and the Restructuring of Neo-Confucianism in the Late Ming* (New York: Columbia University Press, 1986), p. 254. I've changed the romanization in the quotation to *pinyin*.

See also Thomas Metzger's discussion of Zhu Xi and *guan* in *Escape from Predicament,* p. 71.

32. Arieh Lev Breslow, *Beyond the Closed Door,* p. 353.

33. Thomas Metzger, *Escape from Predicament,* p. 116. Douglas Wile, in *Lost T'ai-chi Classics from the Late Ch'ing Dynasty,* p. 158, identifies the *Taijiquan Lun* usage of the *yong li zhi jiu* phrase as an allusion to the fifth chapter of *The Great Learning* (*Da Xue*) on "knowing the root" and the "perfecting of knowledge." In fact, the wording is from Zhu Xi's commentary on the *Da Xue*. See Chan, *A Source Book in Chinese Philosophy,* p. 89; Daniel K. Gardner, *Chu Hsi and the Ta-hsueh: Neo-Confucian Reflection of the Confucian Canon* (Cambridge: Harvard University Press, 1986), pp. 104–105; and James Legge, trans., *The Chinese Classics,* Vol. I (Hong Kong: Hong Kong University Press, 1861–73, Reprint, Taipei: Southern Materials Center, 1985), *The Great Learning,* p. 365.

34. See Allan, *The Way of Water and Sprouts of Virtue,* p. 53, in which she translates the following *Zhuangzi* passage: "When water is still, it reflects one's beard and moustache clearly. Its levelness corresponds to the carpenter's level (*zhun*) and the great craftsman takes his standard from it. If water, when still, is so clear, then how much more the quintessential spirit (*jing shen*). The mind/heart (*xin*) of the sage is clear!"

35. Meng Naichang, *Taijiquan pu yu mipu jiaozhu,* p. 10.

36. James Legge, trans., *The Chinese Classics,* Vol. II, *The Works of Mencius,* IA-8, p. 205. The phrase also appears in the earlier text, *Shang Shu* (Book of Historical Documents): "But to ascertain the views of all; to give up one's own opinion and follow that of others [*she ji cong ren*]; to refrain from oppressing the helpless; and not to neglect the straitened and poor:—it was only the emperor *Yao* who could attain to this." Legge, trans., *The Chinese Classics,* Vol. III, *The Shoo King,* pp. 53–54.

37. Ames, *Sun-tzu: The Art of Warfare,* p. 84. Ames translates the following passage from Chapter 6, p. 127, in *Sunzi*: "As water varies its flow according to (*yin*) the fall of the land, so an army varies its method of gaining victory according to (*yin*) the enemy." The text is conventionally referred to as the *Sun-tzu* (Master Sun), or *Sunzi* in *pinyin*. The full title of this military classic from the Warring States period (c. 403–221 B.C.) is *Sunzi Bingfa* (Master Sun's art of military strategy).

38. T. T. Liang, *T'ai Chi Ch'uan for Health and Self-Defense,* p. 49.

39. See A. C. Graham, *Disputers of the Tao: Philosophical Argument in*

Ancient China (La Salle: Open Court, 1989), pp. 126–127.

40. D. C. Lau, trans., *Mencius* (New York: Penguin, 1970), IIA-2, p. 77. I have changed the romanization to *pinyin*.

41. *Ibid.*

42. *Ibid.* Zheng Manqing (Cheng Man-ch'ing) was well aware of the *Mengzi* passage about *hao ran zhi qi*, and used the phrase in his own "Song of Form and Function" (*Ti Yong Ge*): "The *hao ran zhi qi* (Great *Qi*) can be conducted to the hand."—Benjamin Pang Jeng Lo, trans., *The Essence of T'ai Chi Ch'uan*, p. 94.

43. Legge translates this phrase, "Being nourished by rectitude, and sustaining no injury...," *The Chinese Classics*, Vol. II, p. 190. Allan renders it, "If it is nurtured with straightness and unharmed...," *The Way of Water and Sprouts of Virtue*, p. 91.

44. Quoted in Fung Yu-lan (E. R. Hughes, trans.), *The Spirit of Chinese Philosophy* (Boston: Beacon Press, 1962), p. 27.

45. Lau, *Mencius*, IIA-2, p. 78.

46. Ames, *The Art of Warfare*, p. 129. Interestingly, almost the exact formula appears in the marvelous "Discoursing on Swords" chapter of the *Zhuangzi*. In this story, Zhuangzi is asked to reason with King Wen of Zhao, whose preoccupation with sword fighting causes a decline in his kingdom. Zhuangzi gets his attention by alluding to his own authoritative command of the sword, stating, "The wielder of the sword makes a display of emptiness, draws one out with hopes of advantage, is behindtime in setting out, but beforehand in arriving [*hou zhi yi fa, xian zhi yi zhi*]." Watson, trans., *The Complete Works of Chuang Tzu*, p. 341.

47. Some have even speculated that Wu Yuxiang was also the real author of "The Taijiquan Treatise," but there is no conclusive evidence to prove or disprove this claim. See, for example, T. Y. Pang, *On Tai Chi Chuan* (Bellingham: Azalea Press, 1987), pp. 221, 268–269.

48. Ames, *The Art of Warfare*, p. 158. The Chen Weiming commentary appears in Zeng Zhaoran, *Taijiquan quan shu*, p. 46, and is also discussed in Meng Naichang, *Taijiquan pu yu mipu jiaozhu*, p. 23.

49. See Susan Foe, who in the preface to Benjamin Pang Jeng Lo, *The Essence of T'ai Chi Ch'uan*, p. 7, addresses the difficulty of translating this: "In this context the word which we translate as "excited" has this connotation: if all the oceans in the world were gathered into a box and the box was jiggled, the water would slosh back and forth." Interestingly, this

dang character is the same character that Douglas Wile translates as "swing" for Cheng Man-ch'ing's concept of linkage, or "movement and swing." See Wile, *Cheng Man-Ch'ing's Advanced T'ai-Chi Form Instructions* (New York: Sweet Ch'i Press, 1985), pp. ii-iii, 47, and 62–63.

50. In fact, another Taiji document, Li Yiyu's (1832–1892) "Essentials of the Practice of Form and Push Hands" (*Zou jia da shou xing gong yao yan*), uses the word *jin* in his paraphrase of this classic line: "The *jin* (internal force) rises from the feet, changes in the legs, is stored in the chest, moved in the shoulders and commanded in the waist." From Lo, *The Essence of T'ai Chi Ch'uan*, p. 82, with minor changes. See also Li Yiyu's different paraphrase of the line, again using the word *jin*, in his "Five-Character Secret" (*Wu zi jue*), Lo, p. 76. For a different rendering, plus the original texts, see T.Y. Pang's *On Tai Chi Chuan*, pp. 156–169.

51. Introduction, D.C. Lau and Roger T. Ames, trans., *Yuan Dao: Tracing Dao to Its Source* (New York: Ballantine, 1998), p. 40.

52. *Ibid.*

53. Lau and Ames, trans., *Yuan Dao: Tracing Dao to Its Source*, p. 137.

54. Ames, Introduction, *The Art of Warfare*, p. 71. Ames states on p. 81: "When looked at spatially from outside of one's own 'skin,' *shi* is that set of conditions that is defining of one's situation. It is one's context in relationship to oneself. When looked at from an internal perspective, *shi* is one's own place and posture relative to one's context. When looked at temporally, taking into account the full calculus of dispositions, *shi* is the tension of forces and the momentum that brings one position in immediate contact with another."

55. Ames, *The Art of Warfare*, p. 120.

56. This translation of the title has become something of a convention, and although I follow it here, the actual title, *Da Shou Ge*, would probably be more properly rendered as "Song of Sparring." The term "push hands" is thought to be a relatively recent development in Taijiquan history and is somewhat younger than the training exercise it names.

57. Meng Naichang, *Taijiquan pu yu mipu jiaozhu*, p. 65.

58. Chen Yanlin stresses the importance of "joining" in his description of *ti jin* (lifting energy): "In addition, with regard to direction, proximity, body method and stance, one must in particular join together with the opponent. Otherwise, [the technique] will have no effect; the use of this method must be adapted to circumstances. To get the upper hand

in the use of *ti*, it comes after leading [the opponent]. Then, it matters not which energy (*jin*)—any [of them] could be used to strike, and the opponent will most certainly be dispatched. This is what is meant by the phrase in the Song of Push Hands (*Da Shou Ge*): 'Lead [him] into emptiness, join, then issue.' " From Chen Yanlin, *Taijiquan dao jian gan sanshou hebian* (Taijiquan, saber, sword, staff, and sparring), (Shanghai: 1943), my trans.

59. Lo, trans., *The Essence of T'ai Chi Ch'uan*, p. 81. For original text and a different rendering, see T.Y. Pang, *On Tai Chi Chuan*, pp. 165–169.

60. Lo, *The Essence of T'ai Chi Ch'uan*, p. 82.

61. *Ibid.* The line in *The Art of Warfare* is, "He who knows the enemy and himself will never in a hundred battles be at risk; he who does not know the enemy but knows himself will sometimes win and sometimes lose; he who knows neither the enemy nor himself will be at risk in every battle." Ames, *The Art of Warfare*, p. 113.

附　錄

一、太極拳論

王宗岳

　　太極者無極而生。陰陽之母也。動之則分。靜之則合。無過不及。隨曲就伸。人剛我柔謂之走。我順人背謂之黏。動急則急應。動緩則緩隨。雖變化萬端。而理爲一貫。由着熟而漸悟懂勁。由懂勁而階及神明。然非用力之久。不能豁然貫通焉。虛靈頂勁。氣沉丹田。不偏不倚。忽隱忽現。左重則左虛。右重則右杳。仰之則彌高。俯之則彌深。進之則愈長。退之則愈促。一羽不能加。蠅蟲不能落。人不知我，我獨知人。英雄所向無敵。蓋皆由此而及也。斯技旁門甚多。雖勢有區別。概不外乎壯欺弱。慢讓快耳。有力打無力。手慢讓手快。是皆先天自然之能。非關學力而有爲也。察四兩撥千斤之句。顯非力勝。觀耄耋能御衆之形。快何能爲。立如平准。活似車輪。偏沉則隨。雙重則滯。每見數年純功。不能運化者。率自爲人製。雙重之病未悟耳。欲避此病，須知陰陽。黏卽是走。走卽是黏。陽不離陰。陰不離陽，陰陽相濟。方爲懂勁。懂勁後。愈練愈精。默識揣摩。漸至從心所欲。本是捨己從人。多誤舍近求遠。所謂差之毫厘。謬以千里。學者不可不詳辨焉。是爲論。

　　長拳者。如長江大海。滔滔不絕也。掤攦擠按采挒肘靠。此八卦也。進步退步左顧右盼中定。此五行也。掤攦擠按。卽乾坤坎離四正方也。采挒肘靠。卽巽震兌艮。四斜角也。進退顧盼定。卽金木水火土也。合之則爲十三勢也。

I.

The Taijiquan Treatise

by Wang Zongyue

Taiji, being born of *Wuji*, is the mother of *yin* and *yang*. In movement it differentiates; in stillness it consolidates. It is without excess or insufficiency. Follow, bend, then extend. When the other is hard, and I am soft, this is called yielding. I go along with the other. This is called adhering. To quick movements, I respond quickly. To slow movements, I follow slowly. Although the transformations have innumerable strands, this principle makes them as one thread. From careful investigation and experience, one may gradually realize how to comprehend energy (*dong jin*). From comprehending energy, you will attain by degrees spiritual illumination (*shen ming*). Nevertheless, without an exertion of effort over time (*yong li zhi jiu*), one will not be able to suddenly have a thorough understanding of it.

An intangible and lively energy lifts the crown of the head (*xu ling ding jin*). The *qi* sinks to the *dantian*. No leaning, no inclining. Suddenly hidden, suddenly appearing. When the left feels weight, then the left empties. When the right feels weight, then the right is gone. Looking up, it then becomes yet higher. Looking down, it then becomes yet deeper. Advancing, there is an even longer distance. Retreating, it is then even more crowded. One feather cannot be added. A fly cannot land. The other does not know me; I alone know the other. This is to be a hero with no adversaries along the way. Does it not all come from this?

There are many other kinds of martial arts. Although their forms are distinct from one another, overall they are nothing more than the strong taking advantage of the weak, or merely the slow yielding to the quick. Having strength to strike those without strength, the slow of hand giving way to the quick of hand—these are all from inherent natural ability, and bear no relationship to the capability that comes from earnest study. Examine the expression "Four ounces deflect one thousand pounds." Clearly this is not accomplished by means of strength. Observe a situation in which one who is aged can skillfully fend off (*yu*) a throng. How can this ability be one of speed?

Stand like a balance scale; active, like the wheel of a cart. Sink to one side, then follow. If double weighted (*shuang zhong*), then one will stagnate. Whenever we see those who for several years have perfected their skill, yet are unable to employ this neutralization and are generally overpowered by others, this is merely from not having come to understand the fault of double weighting. If you want to avoid this fault, you must know *yin* and *yang*. To adhere is to yield; to yield is to adhere. *Yang* does not leave *yin*; *yin* does not leave *yang*. The mutual cooperation of *yin* and *yang* is precisely what makes up the understanding of energy (*dong jin*). After comprehending energy, the more the practice, the greater the refinement. Silently memorize (*mo shi*) and ponder (*chuai mo*), and gradually you will attain what you wish from your heart and mind (*cong xin suo yu*). The foundation is to yield to the initiative of the other (*she ji cong ren*). Many mistakenly forsake the near in pursuit of what is far away. It is said: "To be off in one's aim by the slightest fraction, one will lose the target by a thousand miles." The student must therefore be carefully discerning of the details herein. This comprises the treatise.

* * *

What is Long Boxing (*chang quan*)? It is like the Long River, or a great ocean, flowing smoothly and ceaselessly. Ward Off (*peng*), Roll Back (*lu*), Press (*ji*), Push (*an*), Pull Down (*cai*), Rend (*lie*), Elbow Stroke (*zhou*), Shoulder Stroke (*kao*): these are the Eight Trigrams (*ba gua*). Advance, Retreat, Look Left, Gaze Right, Central

Equilibrium: these are the Five Phases (*wu xing*). *Peng, Lu, Ji,* and *An,* accordingly, are [the Trigrams] *Qian, Kun, Kan,* and *Li,* or the four cardinal directions. *Cai, Lie, Zhou,* and *Kao,* then, are [the Trigrams] *Sun, Zhen, Dui,* and *Ken,* or the four corner directions. Advance, Retreat, Look Left, Gaze Right, and Central Equilibrium, accordingly, are Metal, Wood, Water, Fire, and Earth. Taken together, these comprise the Thirteen Postures.

二、十　三　勢　歌

（作者待考）

　　十三總勢莫輕視。命意源頭在腰際。變轉虛實須留意。氣遍身軀不少滯。靜中觸動動猶靜。因敵變化示神奇。勢勢存心揆用意。得來不覺費功夫。刻刻留心在腰間。腹內鬆凈氣騰然。尾閭中正神貫頂。滿身輕利頂頭懸。仔細留心向推求。屈伸開合聽自由。入門引路須口授。功夫無息法自修。若言體用何爲准。意氣君來骨肉臣。想推用意終何在。益壽延年不老春。歌兮歌兮百四十。字字真切義無遺。若不向此推求去。枉費工夫貽歎息。

II.

Song of the Thirteen Postures

Author unknown

The thirteen principal postures are not to be underestimated.
The source of meaning is in the region of the waist.

You must pay attention to the turning transformations of empty and full,
and the *qi* moving throughout your body without the slightest hindrance.

In the midst of stillness one comes in contact with movement, moving as though remaining still.
According with one's opponent, the transformations appear wondrous.

For each and every posture, concentrate your mind and consider the meaning of the applications.
You will not get it without consciously expending a great deal of time and effort (*gongfu*).

Moment by moment, keep the mind/heart (*xin*) on the waist.
With the lower abdomen completely loosened, the *qi* will ascend on its own.

The coccyx (*wei lu*) is centrally aligned, and the spirit (*shen*) threads to the crown of the head.
The whole body is light and nimble when the head is suspended at the crown.

Carefully concentrate upon your study.
The bending, extending, opening and closing: let them come on
　　their own.

Entering the gate and being led to the path, this must come from
　　oral guidance.
To ceaselessly exert oneself (*gongfu wu xi*) in the method is self-
　　cultivation (*zi xiu*).

If you ask, what are the criteria of essence and application?
Intention (*yi*) and *qi* are the authority, the bones and tissues the
　　subjects.

If you want to find out where, in the end, the purpose lies,
it is to increase longevity and extend one's years (*yi shou yan
　　nian*), a springtime of youth.

This song, oh, this song, has one hundred forty words.
Every word is true and concise, there are no omissions.

If inquiry proceeds without regard to this,
one's efforts (*gongfu*) will be wasted, and this will only cause one
　　to sigh with regret.

III.

The Mental Elucidation
of the Thirteen Postures

by Wu Yuxiang

Use the mind/heart (*xin*) to move the *qi*. You must cause it to sink soundly, then it can gather into the bones. Use the *qi* to move the body. You must cause it to accord smoothly, then it can easily follow your mind/heart (*xin*). If the spirit of vitality (*jing shen*) can be raised, then there will be no apprehension of dullness or heaviness. This is what is meant by suspending the crown of the head. The intent (*yi*) and the *qi* must exchange with skillful sensitivity, then you will have a sense of roundness and liveliness. This is what is called the change of insubstantial and substantial. When issuing energy (*fa jin*), one must sink soundly, loosen completely, and focus in one direction. In standing, the body must be centrally aligned, calm and at ease, supporting the eight directions. Move the *qi* as though through a pearl carved with a zigzag path (*jiu qu zhu*, literally, "nine-bend pearl"), reaching everywhere without a hitch. Mobilize *jin* (energy) that is like well-tempered steel, capable of breaking through any stronghold. One's form is like a hawk seizing a rabbit. One's spirit is like a cat seizing a rat. Be still like a mountain, move like a flowing river. Store energy (*xu jin*) as though drawing a bow. Issue energy (*fa jin*) as though releasing an arrow. Seek the straight in the curved. Store up, then issue. The strength issues from the spine; the steps follow the body's changes. To gather in is in fact to release. To break off is to again connect. In going to and fro there must be folding; in advancing and retreating there

三、十三勢行功心解

武禹襄

以心行氣。務令沉着。乃能收歛入骨。以氣運身。務令順遂。乃能便利從心。精神能提得起。則無遲重之虞。所謂頂頭懸也。意氣須換得靈。乃有圓活之趣。所謂變轉虛實也。發勁須沉着鬆淨。專主一方。立身須中正安舒。支撐八面。行氣如九曲珠。無往不利。（氣遍身驅之謂）運勁如百煉鋼。無堅不摧。形如搏兔之鵠。神如捕鼠之貓。靜如山嶽。動如江河。蓄勁如開弓。發勁如放箭。曲中求直。蓄而後發。力由脊發。步隨身換。收卽是放。斷而復連。往復須有折迭。進退須有轉換。極柔軟。然後極堅剛。能呼吸。然後能靈活。氣以直養而無害。勁以曲蓄而有餘。心為令。氣為旗。腰為纛。先求開展。後求緊湊。乃可臻於縝密矣。

又曰。彼不動。己不動。彼微動。己先動。勁似鬆非鬆。將展未展。勁斷意不斷。又曰。先在心。後在身。腹鬆氣歛入骨。神舒體靜。刻刻在心。切記一動無有不動。一靜無有不靜。牽動往來氣貼背。而歛入脊骨。內固精神。外示安逸。邁步如貓行、運勁如抽絲。全身意在精神。不在氣。在氣則滯。有氣者無力。無氣者純剛。氣若車輪。腰如車軸。

must be turning transitions. Arriving at the extreme of yielding softness, one afterward arrives at the extreme of solid hardness. With the ability to inhale and exhale will follow the ability to be nimble and lively. When the *qi* is cultivated in a straightforward manner, there will be no harm. When the energy (*jin*) is stored up in the curves, there will be a surplus. The mind/heart (*xin*) is the commander, the *qi* is the signal flag, the waist is the directional banner. First seek to open and expand, afterwards seek to draw up and gather together, then you will approach refinement.

It is also said, if the other does not move, I do not move. If the other moves slightly, I move first. The energy (*jin*) seems loosened (*song*) yet not loosened; about to expand, but not yet expanding. The energy (*jin*) breaks off, yet the intent (*yi*) does not. It is also said, first in the mind/heart, then in the body. The abdomen is loosened (*song*) so that the *qi* gathers into the bones. The spirit is at ease, the body calm. Carve this, each moment, into your mind/heart; remember closely: when one part moves, there is no part that does not move. When one part is still, there is no part that is not still. Leading the movements to and fro, the *qi* adheres to the back, then collects into the spine. Within, consolidate the spirit of vitality. Without, express tranquillity and ease. Step like a cat walking. Mobilize energy (*jin*) as though drawing silk. Throughout the whole body, the intent (*yi*) is on the spirit of vitality (*jing shen*), not on the *qi*. If it is on the *qi*, then there will be stagnation. One who has it on the *qi* will have no strength. One who does not have it on the *qi* will attain pure hardness. *Qi* is like the wheel of a cart; the waist is like the wheel's axle.

四、太極拳論

武禹襄

一舉動周身俱要輕靈。尤須貫串。氣宜鼓盪。神宜內斂。無使有缺陷處。無使有凸凹處。無使有斷續處。其根在脚。發於腿，主宰於腰。形於手指。由脚而腿而腰。總須完整一氣。向前退後。乃能得機得勢。有不得機得勢處。身便散亂。其病必於腰腿求之。上下前後左右皆然。凡此皆是意。不在外面。有上即有下。有前則有後。有左則有右。如意要向上。即寓下意。若將物掀起而加以挫之之力。斯其根自斷。乃壞之速而無疑。虛實宜分清楚。一處有一處虛實。處處總此一虛實。周身節節貫串。無令絲毫間斷耳。

IV.

The Taijiquan Classic

by Wu Yuxiang

Once in motion, the entire body should be light and agile, and even more importantly, must be threaded together (*guan chuan*). The *qi* should be roused and made vibrant. The spirit (*shen*) should be collected within. Do not allow there to be any protuberances or hollows. Do not allow there to be any intermittence. It is rooted in the feet, issued by the legs, governed by the waist, and expressed in the fingers. From the feet, to the legs, then to the waist, always there must be complete integration into one *qi*. In advancing forward and retreating back, you will then be able to seize the opportunity and the strategic advantage (*de ji de shi*). In a case of not gaining the opportunity and strategic advantage, your body will become scattered and confused. The flaw in this case must certainly be sought in the waist and legs. This is so whether up or down, forward or backward, left or right. These cases are all of mind intent (*yi*) and do not refer to the external. When there is up, then there is down. When there is forward, then there is backward. When there is left, then there is right. If the intent is to go upward, then direct the mind intent downward, just as, if one is going to lift an object, then one in addition applies to it the force of a downward push. Thus, its root will be severed, and it will be collapsed quickly and decisively. Insubstantial and substantial must be clearly distinguished. Each point has its point of insubstantial/substantial. Everywhere there is always this one insubstantial/substantial. The entire body is threaded together joint by joint (*jie jie guan chuan*). Do not allow the slightest interruption.

五、打 手 歌

王宗岳修訂

掤捋擠按須認真。上下相隨人難進。任他巨力來打吾。牽動四兩撥千斤。引進落空合卽出。沾連黏隨不丟頂。

V.

The Song of Pushing Hands

Revised by Wang Zongyue

In Ward Off (*peng*), Roll back (*lu*), Press (*ji*), and Push (*an*),
  you must be conscientious.
Upper and lower follow one another; the other has difficulty
  advancing.

Let him come and strike with great strength.
Lead his movement, using four ounces to deflect a thousand
  pounds.

Attract him into emptiness, join, then issue.
Adhere, connect, stick, follow, without letting go or resisting.

Glossary

an to place the hands on; "push"; one of the primary postures of the Grasp Sparrow's Tail sequence

ban to deflect

cai pull down, "pluck"

dalu big roll back

dantian a point of focus within the lower abdomen located just below the navel; associated with the physical center of gravity

dao the Taiji broadsword

ding dian the culminating point, or ending posture; literally, "fixed point"

fajing issuing energy

fang song to loosen the joints and tissues

gongfu time and labor devoted to an art; efficacious efforts, and the fruits thereof

guan chuan threaded, to penetrate as though with a thread; traditionally this phrase was used to describe strings of coins threaded together for large cash exchanges

he to close, join, unite

heng jin transverse energy, horizontal energy

hu kou "tiger's mouth": the upper opening of the fist, characterized by the surrounding joints of the index finger and the thumb

ji to press, one of the primary postures of the Grasp Sparrow's Tail sequence

jian the Taiji straight sword

jin integrated strength/sensitivity, kinetic energy. In Taijiquan *jin* is contrasted with *li* (strength) or *zhuo li* (crude strength; brute force).

jin dian "energy points": points of concentration that help the practitioner visualize optimal body alignment and directionality of kinetic energy

jin lu "energy path": the pathway of kinetic energy

jing shen vital energy, spirit

kai to open

kai li bu open stance

kao shoulder stroke. I follow convention in this translation. There is nothing etymologically explicit denoting "shoulder" or "stroke" in the character, which means "to rely on, to lean on, to draw near to."

kou verb used to describe the pivoting of a foot on the heel, turning the toes inward

kua thigh; inner thigh, hips

kua gen intersection of the femur with the pelvis; the hip socket

lan to parry

li strength

lie split; a separating out, or spreading action, of the two arms

linghuo lively agility

lu roll back; one of the primary postures of the Grasp Sparrow's Tail sequence

mo to "wipe": verb used to describe hand and arm motions

neiquan internal martial arts

nian to stick

peng ward off; one of the primary postures of the Grasp Sparrow's Tail sequence

pie a verb used to describe the pivoting of a foot on the heel, turning the toes outward

qi breath; matter/energy

qiang the Taiji spear

qu xu "storing up within the curved"

quan fist, boxing art

sanshou free sparring

shen spirit, mental liveliness

shun to go along with; to follow

song loosened, relaxed

tuishou push hands

wei lu the coccyx, tailbone

yao "waist," the lumbar spine and surrounding tissue

yi mind intent

yuandi standing postures

zhou elbow stroke. *Zhou* literally means "elbow." See entry for *kao* regarding convention for translating as "stroke."

zhuo li crude or brute force

Bibliography

Allan, Sarah. *The Way of Water and Sprouts of Virtue*. Albany: State University of New York Press, 1997

Ames, Roger, trans. *Sun-Tzu: The Art of Warfare*. New York: Ballantine Books, 1993

Breslow, Arieh Lev. *Beyond the Closed Door: Chinese Culture and the Creation of T'ai Chi Ch'uan*. Jerusalem: The Almond Blossom Press, 1995

Chan, Wing-tsit. *A Source Book in Chinese Philosophy*. Princeton: Princeton University Press, 1963

Ch'ien, Edward T. *Chiao Hung and the Restructuring of Neo-Confucianism*. New York: Columbia University Press, 1986

Cleary, Thomas, trans. *Mind Over Matter: Higher Martial Arts* by Shi Ming. Berkeley: Frog, Ltd., 1994

Frantzis, Bruce Kumar. *Opening the Energy Gates of Your Body*. Berkeley: North Atlantic Books, 1993

——————. *The Power of Internal Martial Arts: Combat Secrets of Ba Gua, Tai Chi, and Hsing-I*. Berkeley: North Atlantic Books, 1998

Fu Sheng Yuan (author), Fu Zhong Wen (ed.). *Authentic Yang Family Tai Chi: Step by Step Instruction*. Victoria Park: Fu Sheng Yuan International Tai Chi Academy, 1995

Gardner, Daniel K. *Chu Hsi and the* Ta-hsueh: *Neo-Confucian Reflection on the Confucian Canon*. Cambridge: Harvard University Press, 1986

Guttmann, trans. *The T'ai Chi Boxing Chronicle* by Kuo Lien-Ying. Berkeley: North Atlantic Books, 1994

Huang Wen-Shan. *Fundamentals of T'ai Chi Ch'uan*, Third Edition.

Hong Kong: South Sky Book Company, 1979

Jou Tsung Hwa. *The Tao of Tai-Chi Chuan: Way to Rejuvenation,* Fifth Edition. Warwick: Tai Chi Foundation, 1988

Kasulis, Thomas, et al., eds. *Self as Body in Asian Theory and Practice.* Albany: State University of New York Press, 1993

Kjellberg, Paul, and Ivanhoe, Philip J., eds. *Essays on Skepticism, Relativism, and Ethics in the Zhuangzi.* Albany: State University of New York Press, 1996

Lau, D. C., and Ames, Roger T., trans. *Yuan Dao: Tracing Dao to Its Source.* New York: Ballantine Books, 1998

Legge, James. *The Chinese Classics.* Hong Kong: Hong Kong University Press, 1861–73; Reprint, Taipei: Southern Materials Center, 1985

Liang, T. T. *T'ai Chi Ch'uan For Health and Self-Defense: Philosophy and Practice.* New York: Vintage Books, 1974

Lo, Benjamin Pang Jeng, Martin Inn, Robert Amacker, and Susan Foe, trans. and eds., *The Essence of T'ai Chi Ch'uan: The Literary Tradition.* Berkeley: North Atlantic Books, 1979

Meng Naichang. *Taijiquan pu yu mipu jiaozhu* (Taijiquan manuals and secret manuals, annotated). Hong Kong: Hai Feng Chubanshe, 1993

Metzger, Thomas A. *Escape from Predicament: Neo-Confucianism and China's Evolving Political Culture.* New York: Columbia University Press, 1977

Olson, Stuart Alve, trans. *The Intrinsic Energies of T'ai Chi Ch'uan.* St. Paul: Dragon Door Publications, 1994

Pang, T.Y. *On Tai Chi Chuan.* Bellingham, WA: Azalea Press, 1987

Schorre, Jane, and Chang, Margaret. *How to Grasp The Bird's Tail If You Don't Speak Chinese: A Light-Hearted Look at Meaning in Taiji.* Houston, TX: Arts of China Seminars, 1997

Thomas, Howard. *Tai Chi Training in China: Masters, Teachers, and Coaches.* London: Paul H. Crompton Ltd., 1996

Watson, Burton. *The Complete Works of Chuang Tzu.* New York: Columbia University Press, 1968

Wile, Douglas. *Lost T'ai-chi Classics from the Late Ch'ing Dynasty.* Albany: State University of New York Press, 1996

———, trans. *T'ai-chi Touchstones: Yang Family Secret Tranmissions*, Revised ed. Brooklyn: Sweet Ch'i Press, 1983

Wu Kuang-ming, *The Butterfly as Companion: Meditations on the First Three Chapters of the Chuang Tzu.* Albany: State University Press, 1990

Yang Jwing-Ming, *Advanced Yang Style Tai Chi Chuan: Vol. One, Tai Chi Theory and Tai Chi Jing.* Jamaica Plain, NY: YMAA, 1987

Zeng Zhaoran, *Taijiquan quan shu* (Complete Book of Taijiquan). Taibei: Hualian Chubanshe, 1960